THE
VERSATILE
ARABIAN
HORSE

ROSEMARY ARCHER

J. A. ALLEN · LONDON

British Library cataloguing in publication data
A catalogue record for this book is available from
the British Library

ISBN 0-85131-669-7

Published in Great Britain in 1996 by
J. A. Allen & Company Limited
1 Lower Grosvenor Place
London SW1W 0EL

Typeset by Textype Typesetters, Cambridge
Printed by Dah Hua Printing Press Co., Hong Kong

Edited by Elizabeth O'Beirne-Ranelagh
Designed by Paul Saunders

Contents

Acknowledgements

The author would like to thank Kat Waldon and Gudrun Waiditschka for kindly sending much information from the U.S.A. and Europe. Also Jennifer Ashton of the Arabian Jockey Club, Vreni Riedler, Charmaine Grobbelaar, Mary Lockwood, Vicki Maclean, Margo Portman, Betty Finke, Helen Knight, Jacquie Webby, Lorraine Vickers, Britta Fahlgren, Doris Melzer, Toni Kylstra-Tissot van Patot, Marion Winkler, Louise Hermelin, Tina Karlsson, Gunilla Wolde, Gabrielle Hammerer, G. Hussman, Professor P. A. Boyazoglu, Jaco de Klerk, Carlin Nicole, Marina Groner, Eduardo Usandivaras, Nies Dreyer and Pam Brown, all of whom gave valuable help by providing information and some of the photographs, and to the Arab Horse Society for their kind assistance and use of their Library. Especial thanks to Diana Dykes without whose expertise and help in preparing the manuscript this book might never have been completed.

Thanks also to the following for the use of their photographs: Eric Jones, Betty Finke, Judith Ratcliff, Pat Slater, Marilyn and Peter Sweet, Trevor Meekes, Christine Massey and John Brett. Also to Stella Walker, Monica Calvert, Pat Coward, Beatrice Paine, Marianne Løwe, Lynne Whittaker, Denniss Hulme, Patricia Lindsay, Catherina Nelson, Bazy Tankersley, David Nye, Bob Marshall, Julia Wynmalen, Deirdre Robinson, Jane Kadri and Gillian Lancaster who kindly loaned photographs. The cover photograph is of Aboud (Diamond Star ex Azeme Bint Gleam) by Gillian Lancaster.

Introduction

DURING THE SECOND half of the twentieth century the population of Arabian horses outside their land of origin has grown astronomically. In the U.K., where up until the Second World War only a handful of studs contained more than half a dozen Arabians, there are now several with 50 to over 100. Together with the hundreds of 'small' breeders producing a few foals annually, the total number born each year in the U.K. has averaged around 1,000 in recent years. This same pattern is repeated in most Arab horse-breeding countries in the world and, more recently, in addition some Arab sheikhs have been acquiring and breeding an increasing number.

Some people consider this population explosion has been good for the breed, inasmuch as it demonstrates popularity. Others see disadvantages and are concerned for the future of the Arabian. Where there is a marked increase in birth-rate there is a likelihood of the element of indiscriminate or thoughtless breeding. There are also other problems.

Prior to the Second World War only a few shows held classes for Arab horses; there are now a large number which cater for them, attracting many entrants. Competition is high and current trends in in-hand showing appear to reveal that for some the main considerations are following fashion and breeding for the show-ring only. The pretty, 'typey' horse shown in the modern 'flamboyant' style is more likely to catch the eye, but some lack good sound legs and feet and throughout the world there are Arabians in the show-ring today which are deemed unsuitable for ridden work, a state of affairs which can lead detractors to condemn the breed as a whole.

On the other hand, there is a danger of losing some of the quality and beauty of the Arabian if bred specifically for performance ability. The ideal to be aimed for is the horse which can compete with equal success in-hand and in performance. Examples of Arabians which meet this ideal are presented in these pages.

Not enough has been done to show the world at large just how capable the Arab horse is of holding his own in open competition. The main purpose of this book is to draw attention to the diverse events these horses compete in today and it is hoped that there will follow a greater understanding and acknowledgement of the breed's exceptional qualities as an all-round performer.

Many instances of individual Arabians, as well as Anglo-Arabs and part-breds, which have achieved outstanding performances appear in the following pages; but the sheer number of successful horses has regrettably led to many worthy of mention having to be omitted.

CHAPTER ONE

The Arabian in warfare and ancient sports

THE DESERT ANCESTORS of our present-day Arabians were used primarily by the Bedouin as war horses. They were eminently suited for the battles and raids between warring tribes because of their unique qualities of endurance, agility, courage and speed – this last being the essence of the Arabian, for it is the fastest pure old breed, the Thoroughbred and Quarter Horse having been evolved from an admixture of Oriental and other blood.

Much has already been written on the antiquity of the Arabian and on the different theories put forward as to its exact origin. What is not in question, however, is that it is the most ancient pure breed in existence, and that even before the first mention of horses in Arabia itself there is evidence of animals of distinct Arabian type throughout the Middle and Near East. These Eastern horses are acknowledged to be the tap-root stock of all hot-blooded equines, as opposed to the cold-blooded Northern animals of a much heavier and coarser build.

It is claimed that a pebble engraving found on the coast of Southern Turkey which shows a running or leaping horse of characteristic Arabian type dates from roughly 8000 B.C. At a later date jewellery and other artefacts of around 1600 B.C. depicted 'slender, graceful and fiery' horses, whilst the earliest representations of horses in Egyptian art at around this time also show horses with Arabian characteristics.

Some of the oldest evidence of working horses of this type shows them pulling light chariots, for chariot-racing was one of the earliest equine sports. Another was a form of ball game. The *Encyclopaedia Britannica* mentions a reference in the *Alexiad* of Anna Comnena (about A.D. 1120) to a game played on horseback in which a staff, curved at the end and strung with strips of plaited gut, was used. It also states that 'good authorities also find a more ancient derivation of the game in Egypt, in Persia and among the Arabs before Charlemagne' (born 742 or 3).

These references refer to the origins of tennis, described as an independent member of the family of ball games of which 'the parent root was probably buried in Egypt or Persia 500 years before the Christian era'.

Equally this could be said of polo, acknowledged to be one of the most ancient of games with stick and ball. Persian manuscripts show clearly this sport being played with horses of very distinct Arabian type in the tenth century.

It is easy to appreciate that for racing and sports in which agility and handiness were essential, Arabians were far superior to the rather heavier type of earlier times, such as the Parthian horses.

Accounts of Arab warfare given by travellers to Arabia in the nineteenth century explain how mares were nearly always used on forays into enemy camps as they were less likely than stallions to raise an alarm by whinnying. The Bedouin would ride their camels (which also provided milk for the Arabs and their mares) on long distances, leading the war mares which would be kept fresh for the raids. Speed was essential to enable them to get away from pursuing enemies and the fastest mares became desert celebrities.

An Arab carrying the long Bedouin lance.

Their mounts also had to be strong and agile, for in battle the Arabs used to carry long lances. The horses had to endure all the hardships of desert life, with its extremes of heat and cold, and often on scanty rations. The courage and toughness of the Arabian was thus tested to the full.

A notable traveller, Wilfrid Blunt, was in a unique position to sum up 'the peculiar qualities of the Arab' for, with his wife Lady Anne, he had journeyed extensively amongst the horse-breeding tribes of Arabia during the late 1870s and early 1880s, when acquiring mares and stallions for their stud in England. They got to know the leaders of the tribes and with Lady Anne's fluency in Arabic they attained great knowledge of the breed.

In an article 'About Arab Horses – an Interview with Mr Wilfrid Blunt', which appeared in the *Pall Mall Gazette* of 16 July 1889, Blunt, when asked about his intentions with regard to breeding Arab horses, replied that he would be 'keeping the breed pure and developing the peculiar qualities of the Arab, which are (1) perfect soundness, especially in the legs and feet, where English horses are most defective; (2) good temper (they have not got such a thing as a kick in

them); (3) beauty; and (4) staying power'. In reply to the question 'To what purposes is the Arab best fitted in England?' Blunt says:

Ibn Saud's stud at Sulaimiya (Kharj).

He is very useful as a hack, but you must not suppose that he is not capable of carrying very heavy weights in that capacity. Then he is a very bold performer across country . . . He is perhaps still better adapted for light carriage work, owing to the excellence of his feet, which will stand any amount of wear and tear. He is a good trotter, and will preserve an even pace up the steepest hills . . . The special characteristics of the Arab may be traced to the circumstances and necessities of Bedouin life. The great intellectual development, if I may use the word, and the great docility of temper, clearly come from selection by breeders who live in daily companionship with their horses. The Bedouin children are all day running about and playing among the heels of the mares. The breeders would therefore discard an awkward or ill-tempered beast, and by a long process of selection get rid of ill temper. Again, great hardness of constitution is necessary in a country which is subject to droughts, dearths, and violent change of climate . . . The Bedouin system of warfare, which is the purpose to which they are put, accounts for their enormous staying power. It consists of long forced marches often of as much as five hundred miles, where they would be obliged to do as much as fifty to eighty miles per day, on no better food than chances to come in their way, and often without water. Then at the end they must have sufficient courage and spirit left to be able to manoeuvre in Arab lance fighting and to carry their masters back with the booty they have secured . . .

Wilfrid Blunt remarks on changes noticeable in the late nineteenth century:

> During the last twenty-five years great numbers of Arab brood mares have left Arabia, the Bedouins having been seduced from their ancient practice of never selling a mare by the high prices offered by Abbas Pasha when Viceroy of Egypt. The introduction of fire-arms into Bedouin warfare, too, has tended to diminish the stock; whereas formerly a well mounted Arab could ride into the enemy's camp, pillage, and retire with impunity, he is now at the mercy of any old woman who can catch up a rifle. The system of warfare is yearly changing, and expeditions on dromedaries are replacing those on horseback. A fleet horse is no longer a fortune to its possessor.

The writer of the article sums up his interview with Mr Blunt in the following words:

> From which it would appear, concluded I, when I had taken my departure, that the future of the Arab will be laid in other lands and under other conditions. But of this we may be certain – that the wonderful combination of qualities infused into their horses by these fierce marauders, the patience and the strength, the matchless grace and nobleness of bearing will not be lost; that, as it took ages to produce him, so he will go down through the centuries no less beautiful and perfect than we find him today.

War horses

Some of the earliest desert-bred Arabians to be registered in the General Stud Book (G.S.B.) had been used in warfare before coming to England. Amongst those imported by Wilfrid and Lady Anne Blunt as foundation stock for their Crabbet Stud, the chestnut Rodania had been the war mare of the Roala Sheikh, Sotamm Ibn Shaalan. Rodania was celebrated in the desert and was the cause of a family feud when Sotamm's cousin Beneyeh Ibn Shaalan had taken the mare by force when her breeder refused to sell her. She bred three fillies at Crabbet and was the foundress of what is probably the largest family of pure-bred Arabians in the world.

One of the Blunt's earliest purchases in the desert, the bay stallion Kars, had survived a war whose battles involved firearms. They bought him in 1878 from Mahmud Aga, a Kurdish Chief of an irregular cavalry force raised in the Northern desert during the Russian war. Lady Anne described how in 1877 Mahmud Aga had ridden Kars in the war in Armenia where nearly every horse perished.

On one occasion Kars was struck by a bullet on the inside of the cannon bone, knocking him over, and he and his rider rolled several yards. He was wounded a second time when shot, described as an inch in diameter, hit his shoulder. On the retreat from Armenia to Aleppo Kars appeared to be so exhausted that his saddle and bridle were taken off and he was left behind, but he got up again and followed his master. Both reached Aleppo in such a wretched state that recovery seemed doubtful. Kars was also suffering from a very sore back; he was fired on the belly as a counter-irritant and it was some time before he was considered out of danger. He was only just recovering in Aleppo when the Blunts purchased him.

Less than three months after his arrival in England Kars ran in a hurdle race over two miles at Streatham. Despite being given a high weight he ran well and finished only some seven lengths behind the winner in a fast-run race. Three years later Wilfrid Blunt wrote that Kars, who was only 14.2½ hh, was a brilliant jumper and carried his 13 stone with ease. He hunted him frequently with the Southdown and said that Kars had 'never been beaten or stopped by any fence'.

Another well-known stallion registered in the G.S.B. who had been a war horse was Maidan, who went from Arabia to Bombay in 1871. Since the Bedouin used mares in warfare there were always many surplus colts and most were bought by townspeople who sold them on. One of the largest markets for Arabian stallions at that time was India where there was a good demand for them as chargers for British army officers, and also for racing and other sports.

Maidan was purchased by Lt Colonel Brownlow who rode him in campaigns through India and Afghanistan. Colonel Brownlow was killed commanding his troops at Kandahar in 1880 and Maidan was sold. Over the next few years he won many races in India, including the Ganges Hog Hunt Cup and a four-mile steeplechase. He also won the Kadir cup, the major pigsticking trophy. When nearly 20 years old Maidan was purchased by the Hon. Eustace Vesey who brought him to England where he was again successfully raced, was hunted in Suffolk, and won a steeplechase at the age of 22. Maidan ended his adventurous life with the Hon. Miss Dillon who bred several foals by him before his death in 1892, so that his name appears in the pedigrees of many present-day horses.

These three were all registered animals but there have been many other pure-bred Arabian war horses, as well as all those of distinct Arabian type but not authenticated, or of very largely Arabian blood.

A number of these horses, like Maidan, became officers' chargers and were later brought back to England after campaigns in India. Particularly well-known was Vonolel, a grey purchased in Bombay as a two year old by Lord Roberts in 1877. For 13 years Vonolel was a charger and he took part in the 313-mile forced march from Kabul to Kandahar in 1880. By special permission of Queen Victoria Vonolel was decorated with the Kabul Medal and Kabul-Kandahar Star and he was ridden by Lord Roberts in the Queen's Diamond Jubilee Parade. Vonolel was buried in the garden of the Royal Hospital in Dublin. In paintings he is depicted as a high-class Arabian.

Many of the officers who took part in the battles in Egypt and Sudan in the 1880s and 1890s also rode Arabians. S.A.H.A.A. Imam in *The Centaur* writes of Winston Churchill's description of the embarkation of his regiment at Cairo on their way to join Kitchener's forces near Khartoum in 1898 in his book *The River War*. Their horses were Arabian stallions and loading them into cattle trucks caused considerable commotion. 'But perseverance overcomes everything, even the vivacity of the little Arab horse, though at times he seems to be actually infected with the fanaticism of the human inhabitants of the land of his birth.' Churchill said the grey stallion he rode in the cavalry charge at Omdurman was 'as active as a cat' and 'just slipped into and out of a nullah' which suddenly loomed under them during the charge.

Yet another story is told of how one desert-bred stallion, the chestnut Bashom who was only 14.1 hh, galloped 50 miles in one afternoon bearing vital despatches before the battle of Omdurman. He collapsed with exhaustion and was left for dead but by the next morning had recovered. Bashom was wounded at Omdurman and was later imported to England by Captain W. Smythe.

Captain Honoure de Montmorency, who won a Victoria Cross in the Sudan, rode Parahk, a 14 hh Arabian, and there are many others whose history has not been fully recorded.

Undoubtedly the most famous chargers were the two stallions belonging to Napoleon and Wellington – Marengo and Copenhagen respectively. Napoleon, in fact, had a number of Arab chargers, including the white mare Marie, Wagram, and Gallipoli and Godolphin, two grey Arabs used in Percheron breeding. Jaffa, a grey Arabian obtained by Napoleon in Egypt, eventually came to England; one account was that he was acquired by a Frenchman who, between 1815 and 1830, rented Glassenbury Park, Cranbrook, Kent, in the grounds of which the horse is buried with an

Marengo, Napoleon's charger at Waterloo. (By James Ward, lithograph published in 1824)

inscription on the Wealden stone which marks the spot: 'Under this stone lies Jaffa, the famous charger of Napoleon, aged 37 years.'

Another mare, Tauris, is described as a silver grey with white mane and tail and she is said to be the horse Napoleon rode in Russia, where she became very lame and 'a special "vet" was employed to look after her'. She was also reputed to be Napoleon's second horse at Waterloo when Marengo was wounded in the foot.

Marengo was Napoleon's favourite charger and it is he who is depicted most often in equestrian paintings of the great man. He was named after the battle in Italy when a brilliant cavalry charge gave Napoleon complete victory and ensured his military renown.

Sources conflict as to the exact identity of Marengo. One opinion is that he was bred in Ireland and was by Hidalgo, a son of Eclipse, out of a mare called Vagary. Eclipse, of course, carried much Arabian blood, being descended from all the three main foundation sires of the Thoroughbred, the Godolphin Arabian, the Darley Arabian and the Byerley Turk. In addition to these three stallions there were many other Eastern horses in the foundation stock of the Thoroughbred and many of their early descendants showed true Arab type.

Marengo was said to have been sold to a French officer and taken to Egypt where, according to Juliet McLeod, some time after the battle of Aboukir in July 1799, he became one of Napoleon's chargers.

Other sources maintain that Marengo was a pure-bred Arab. What is certain is that Marengo was acquired in Egypt by Napoleon and that he took part in many battles until his last – Waterloo in 1815 – after which he was captured by the English and brought to England by Lord Petre. He was sold to Lt General Angerstein, and stood at his stud in Cambridgeshire until 1821 at a fee of 10 guineas. Marengo lived to a great age and his well-preserved skeleton was seen by Juliet McLeod in the National Army Museum at Sandhurst. She writes in the *Arab Horse Society News* (Spring 1965) that it was in excellent condition, and particularly notes the fine quality and density of bone, long sloping pasterns ending in splendid little feet, with the horn fine-grained and hard (one had been made into a snuff box and was in St James's Palace). His thigh from stifle to hock was of remarkable length; the skull fine and roomy without heaviness, the jaws deep and well apart at the throat; the mouth bars long and the eye orbit low and definitely round – all hallmarks of the Arabian, added to which Marengo was only 14.1 hh. He sired no notable racehorses, but all his foals are said to have inherited his grey colour and to have been of distinct Arabian type.

The chestnut Copenhagen was a grandson of Eclipse and although he does not appear to have been as beautiful as Marengo, he showed strong Arabian characteristics – and was certainly not lacking in character! So much has been written about the Duke of Wellington that inevitably there are many anecdotes about his famous charger.

Copenhagen is described in the official guide booklet for Stratfield Saye (the estate Wellington chose to buy with the money voted to him by a grateful nation after his victory at Waterloo) as being 15 hh. His dam was a mare belonging to Lord Grosvenor, under whose command Wellington took part in the 1807 expedition to capture the Danish fleet in Copenhagen harbour. She was apparently found to be in foal when the expedition arrived and was sent home; although another version of the story states that she carried General Grosvenor at the siege of Copenhagen before returning to England. The colt foal born in 1808 was later bought by Wellington and named Copenhagen.

In Brian Vesey-Fitzgerald's *The Book of the Horse* Copenhagen is given as being by Meteor, by Eclipse, out of Lady Catherine, but 'his name was removed from the Stud Book when it was discovered his grand-dam was a hunter'. In 1811 Copenhagen ran at Newmarket in General Grosvenor's colours but he 'was not a great success on the turf'.

Whatever his exact pedigree and racing ability may have been, Copenhagen was obviously a brilliant charger. Lady Longford quoted Wellington as saying, 'There may have been many faster horses, no doubt many handsomer, but for bottom and endurance I never saw his fellow.' He was the Duke's favourite charger and carried him throughout the Peninsular campaign and at Waterloo.

An excerpt from *The Great Duke* by Arthur Bryant gives the following account: 'It was eleven o'clock before the victor dismounted outside the inn at Waterloo. As he patted the horse which had borne him so patiently all day, Copenhagen made his commentary on the terrible battle through which he had passed by suddenly lashing out and breaking free.' A footnote adds: 'It took a groom half an hour to catch him.'

After the campaign Copenhagen was often ridden by one or other of Wellington's female admirers. In Paris one year Lady Shelley ('more interested in Wellington than Paris') 'attended a review with Wellington

Copenhagen, ridden by the Duke of Wellington throughout the battle of Waterloo. (Lithograph from James Ward's oil painting)

and rode Copenhagen, the fine chestnut charger which had carried the Duke at Waterloo', wrote John Fisher in *Eighteen Fifteen*.

Later Lady Shelley was in Vienna and, according to Philip Guedalla in *The Duke*, Wellington wrote to her that he 'missed his "absent" A.D.C. at the reviews'. Other belles rode Copenhagen, amongst them Georgy Lennox, who

> found him a rather trying mount from an unpleasing mannerism of neighing violently at the sight of troops (an authentic instance of a warhorse laughing 'ha-ha' to the trumpeters); and one day when she found herself in a square with him, she overheard the ranks remarking: 'take care of that 'ere horse; he kicks out; we knew him well in Spain' . . .

Copenhagen probably mellowed with age and demonstrated the Arabian characteristic of gentleness with children, because during his long and honourable retirement at Stratfield Saye he was 'frequently ridden by the Duke and a multitude of children including Wellington's grand-children'. He died there in 1836 at the age of 28 and was buried with military honours. The headstone erected over him gives the following: 'Here lies Copenhagen the charger ridden by the Duke of Wellington the entire day at the Battle of Waterloo. Born 1808, died 1836', and underneath are the lines:

> God's humbler instrument, though meaner clay
> Should share the glory of that glorious day.

CHAPTER TWO

Selection and basic training for performance work

THE SELECTION of an Arabian for performance work is not very different from choosing a horse of any other breed. The basic need is for good conformation, combined with the special characteristics inherent in Arabians: their quality, which is shown particularly in the beautiful head with large eyes, delicately shaped nostrils and fineness of bone structure, the fine texture of mane and tail, the elegance and high tail carriage. Additionally Arabians have exceptional intelligence, evidenced in their lively expression and behaviour. The toughness and courage of the breed is apparent when they are in hard work.

For endurance a horse of around 15 hands is considered to be the best, with good depth through the heart, and a well-developed chest. A clean, wide throat-latch ensures good wind passage. The shoulder should be well laid back, the ribs well sprung. The quarters should be strong and muscular to give driving power. Good legs are an obvious requirement, showing muscular forearms, large flat knees, and short strong cannon bones with the tendons clearly defined. Hocks should be well let down, strong and neither too close nor bent, and thighs strong and muscular.

Possibly of the greatest importance for an endurance horse is its hooves. 'No foot, no horse' is as true now as it ever was, and the feet should be very carefully examined as endurance horses have to work over all kinds of going. Hooves should be round, not of excessive size, nor small, pinched or boxy. The sole should be arched or concave, not flat and dropped, as this gives too close contact with the ground. The wall should be thick, and the frog deep and wide at the heel.

The ideal angle from coronet to the ground is 45 degrees. The hoof angle is normally repeated in the slope of pastern and shoulder, so that the working of hooves, legs and shoulders is closely interrelated. This slope is important for a smooth ride and minimal leg concussion. If the pasterns are too short this could result in jarring and if too long it is a weakness.

The action is important and is also linked with conformation. Natural good carriage is desired, with free airy movement. A long free, elastic stride gives a comfortable trot and canter. Arabians often widen their hind leg track when trotting fast and this prevents overreach. Horses which have a tendency to forge, brush, overreach or knock themselves should be avoided.

Careful consideration should be given to temperament, for in endurance work in particular rapport between horse and rider is very important. Ann Hyland's sound advice in her book *The Endurance Horse* is to pick a horse you can work with harmoniously. Another comment she makes, equally valid, is that show-ring successes are not always indicative of suitability, as judgement is of outward appearance, sometimes in gross condition which can hide a multitude of faults at first glance.

Ann Hyland writes of a very interesting experiment, conducted at Kansas State University, which was reported in *Equus* Magazine. The object was to determine what makes certain horses perform to exceptionally high standards.

Lesley Caswell and Archimedes (Ahmoun ex Kamisha), who was still competing at the age of 17 in 1994. In 1980 he was British National Champion gelding; he has been in the Endurance Horse and Pony Society top ten several times and was the second horse in the history of the society to complete over 4,000 competitive miles.

The experiment consisted of using a high-speed treadmill (capable of making horses produce speeds of over 30 m.p.h.) to test racehorses, particularly Quarter Horse sprinters; but it was a pure-bred Arabian, Dana's North Lite, with an excellent record in 50 and 100-mile rides, which was first used for a study on endurance.

Using the treadmill enabled cardiovascular studies of horses under stress to be made, recording the biochemical changes whilst they were actually happening. Following the treadmill tests, Dana's North Lite was given a ten-mile gallop, before and after which his temperature, heart and respiration rate were taken, together with blood samples and muscle biopsies. It was determined that 'the main elements of the sustained aerobic work were his cardiovascular system, his muscles, and his ability to eliminate waste'. Two other Arabians were also tested as a comparison.

The tests proved that the Arabians were superior to the Quarter Horses in essential qualities for endurance work. Dana's North Lite's ability to eliminate waste so efficiently was the result of training, as was the ability to utilise to the maximum all the inherited factors – a more efficient heart, superior blood composition, endurance-orientated muscle fibre. There is no doubt that the inherent qualities of the Arabian have proved it to be the supreme breed for endurance riding.

For racing, or most other work, size is usually more a matter of taste than necessity. A tall rider will probably feel happier on a larger horse. Some very good Arab racehorses have been quite small, and in racing the real test only

Saker, by Ahmoun out of Moulton Star, British National Junior Male Champion as a three year old in 1988. A winner and consistently well placed in three seasons' racing, including third in the Dunhill Sprint at Kempton in 1990.

comes when the horse is actually in competition on the course. However, the basic guidelines are the same as those for choosing horses for endurance.

Although Arab racing in the U.K. has not existed long enough for particular blood-lines to stand out consistently for their speed, certain lines are just beginning to emerge as pre-eminent. In Russia and Poland, where racing is used as a test of toughness and mentality to decide selection of breeding stock, some lines are already known for their successes on the race-track. The French have selected for speed for over 100 years, and type has been secondary to performance.

A note of warning might not come amiss at this stage of the progress of Arab racing, which is rapidly becoming a very popular sport in many countries. If Arabians are bred solely for their speed we risk losing some of the unique attributes of the breed – beauty, gentleness with courage, and supreme staying power. Wilfrid Blunt, with his knowledge of Arabians in their desert home, and as a breeder in England, wrote that the Arabian as a breed was as near perfection as one could get, and to breed exclusively for any one quality, whether it be speed or beauty, was folly and would prove detrimental as it would upset the whole equilibrium. In my opinion his

Europejczyk by El Pas out of Europa, Polish National Champion. A Derby winner and unbeaten on the race-track.

counsels should be acted upon by all breeders in order to preserve the Arabian and keep him as nature made him.

One of the most important features of a good performance horse is mentality. For those about to look for a young horse to train for any discipline it is advisable to visit a number of studs and note the general character of the inmates. The performance record of horses bred at the stud, or of similar breeding at other studs, is also a useful guide. A pattern of consistency in a group of closely related animals is likely to indicate their ability. This is not a golden rule, of course, as there are exceptions in every family, but it is a guide for the beginner to follow.

A love of jumping seems to run in families as do some less desirable characteristics such as a reluctance to go through water, often resulting in jumping over puddles! However, such minor problems can usually be overcome easily, and an Arabian which has been well brought up from its earliest days will become a delightful ride if trained well.

Training begins almost immediately after the foal is born. The early days are important as the young foal learns to trust and obey humans. Foals handled with kindness and firmness grow into good-mannered, willing horses. Of course they have some spirit and lessons have to be learned, but these can be accomplished without tears if sensible training is followed.

We like to 'cradle' our newly born foals from the very first time they come out of their loose-box with their mother. This is done by holding them with one arm round the chest and the other round the hindquarters. A stable rubber held round the neck can be used if preferred, instead of holding it with an arm.

Provided it has been a normal and easy birth, the foal is strong and healthy and the weather good, this first outing can be taken when the foal is 24 to 48 hours old. The best place is a small paddock where the mare can be held to graze whilst the foal has freedom to move around in safety. There is nothing more entrancing than watching a foal during its first few outings into the world outside its stable. It will often stop to investigate its body, sniffing and feeling its legs, sides, or even trying to catch its tail – very young foals appear almost as supple as cats! Then realisation dawns on it that it has been supplied with limbs that can move quite fast and in less than no time it will begin cantering round its dam. The ability and the astuteness in changing legs which it rapidly develops never cease to amaze. However, there are also a few tumbles when corners are taken too sharply at speed and care should be taken if the ground is wet and slippery. An indoor school is useful when the weather is bad.

We start teaching the foal to be led with a headcollar on though at first still with an arm round its neck or quarters according to whether the foal is

Mare and foal in a large, well-shaded paddock.

one which goes forward easily or not. Personally I do not like leaving headcollars on foals, or indeed on horses of any age – I have heard of fatal accidents should they get caught up. If a headcollar has to be left on it is advisable to have the type which will break in an emergency.

If the headcollar is worn whilst the foal is led out to the paddock and then taken off and the foal let loose it will learn that when the headcollar is on it must obey its handler, but when removed it is free to play. We bring up our foals this way and always teach them to be caught in the field and the headcollar put on again for the return to the stable. Sometimes this needs patience if a foal decides to have a game of 'catch me if you can'! But we have found that foals reared this way more readily obey halter lessons at a later stage.

Foals should be well handled and taught from an early age to have their feet picked up in readiness for when the blacksmith starts to pare them. Training on the halter, teaching to stand and later to trot out, continues as the foal grows up. Of course extra time must be spent if it is to be shown in hand and it is always useful to train horses early to go happily into a trailer or horse-box. This basic training, which should be the rule with all young horses, should prepare any Arabian for the more serious work of becoming a performance horse.

Arabians are slow to mature. To force them as yearlings, or at any age, and to feed them up so they become fat or heavy young animals, is harmful and can lead to many problems. Their bones need to develop slowly, as nature intended, and leg complaints can easily develop when hard work begins if they have been forced as youngsters. A young horse which has been over fat takes far longer to become fit when training begins, and much greater care has to be taken before introducing fast work, or even hard slower work.

The best recipe for rearing Arabians is to allow them plenty of fresh air and freedom. Larger paddocks where they can really stretch their legs and enjoy a good gallop are preferable to small enclosures. They should be stabled at night through the worst of the winter weather, and fed hay and hard food, care being taken to ensure they have a correct diet according to each individual and the land on which they graze. During the summer they should live out all the time.

Arabians do not take happily to a life of being over restricted to their stables and having insufficient exercise. This aspect is perhaps something which is not fully understood and if problems with an Arabian stallion arise more often than not it is due to the horse not having been allowed sufficient freedom. I have heard an overseas owner remark on the good temperament of stallions living happily with an ample paddock in which to run out, adding, 'How can one expect the same good nature to be shown by stallions kept permanently "caged up" in a barn?'

At three years of age the serious work can begin with lungeing and long reining as preparation for backing. Lungeing is useful for toning muscles and for teaching the young horse to regulate his stride and promote suppleness. Working on a lunge is more strenuous than straight work and care should be taken to circle an equal length of time each way, and never for too long a time altogether. At this stage the horse can be taught to listen to commands, to rein back and to stand still.

There are numerous good books on the rearing and training of horses and it is not intended here to go into detail on these subjects since they could fill another whole book. Henry Wynmalen's *Horse Breeding and Stud Management* and *Equitation* cover all aspects of raising foals and initial training and are written by an exponent thoroughly sympathetic to the

The ten-year-old stallion, Istfahan, enjoying the freedom of his paddock. By Aurelian out of Istashra, Istfahan won races in 1992 and 1993. His show record includes major wins and two reserve championships. He was also awarded 88.8 points and a Gold Medal at the 1995 Towerlands International.

An alert and interested young stallion out on exercise: Rusleem at four years old.

needs of the Arabian, with its high intelligence and sensitivity. Arabians tend to get bored quickly and a lesson once learned should never be hammered home by constant repetition, for this can irritate.

It should be stated that sometimes a horseman will find himself at odds with these qualities of the breed, and unable to appreciate fully the individualistic nature. However, people often say that once they have owned and ridden an Arabian they could never go back to another breed.

Being a slow maturing breed serious hard work should not start before the age of four. No horses are allowed to run in Arab racing in Britain until they are four years old and this is a very wise rule of the Arab Horse Society. Rules for long distance and endurance riding are also wisely made and horses have to be even older than this before they can move on to the longer endurance rides.

Ideally, young Arabians should be backed as three-year-olds and then allowed to rest until they are four. Lessons can then begin where they were left off the previous year, with a gradual increase in the length of time ridden and work undertaken. Physical and mental make-up help to determine each individual's preparation, for they all differ, but as a general rule the horse

ABOVE *Biru Tarkaroi, by Ringing Gold out of Makarish, ridden by Philip Nye in Tasmania, demonstrating complete trust and understanding between horse and rider.*

Fully trained gelding, Hal, by Ibn El Hamra out of Opal, ridden by Kim Lowe in the dressage section of eventing.

27

should be kept interested, relaxed and yet alert. This aspect of the horse's training is admirably described in detail by Henry Wynmalen in *Equitation*.

For more advanced training Anne Hyland's *The Endurance Horse* gives detailed information for those who wish to go in for this sport. Many Arab racehorses have preparation similar to the endurance horse for the early part of their training before moving on to fast work. Racehorse training is also a specialised subject and it is recommended that those who decide to take up racing seek advice from a good trainer. Once into any kind of specialist work it is obviously best to consult and learn from experts.

CHAPTER THREE

The history of Arab racing

A resumé of early Arab racing

In a previous chapter it was mentioned that the Arabian is the swiftest pure breed. The Thoroughbred, of mixed ancestry and having been developed specifically for racing, is faster. Quarter Horses (also of mixed ancestry) are fast over short distances and can even outrun the Thoroughbred for a few hundred yards, but they cannot keep it up for long. Quarter Horses are usually raced over distances of less than half a mile, when they go flat out from start to finish, and it is on the basis of these short runs that they gained their reputation of being the 'fastest' breed.

Arabians are seldom pitted against Thoroughbreds but on the rare occasions that they have run against them only over very long distances have they won. The 1938 *Journal of the Arab Horse Society* contains an account, taken from the *Egyptian Gazette* of 9 February 1888, of the celebrated match between Mr Smart's English racer and Prince Halim's Arab, it was believed for £10,000, from Cairo to Suez and back.

A well-known English jockey was engaged to ride the English horse and a native jockey rode the Arab. The distance is *roughly 160 miles*. The English horse started at a great pace and soon lost the Arab, arriving at Suez some 35 miles ahead. There the horse was put up and fed and the jockey, after a good meal, went to bed. An hour or two later the Arab arrived and the jockey was woken up, but he remarked that if he were called in an hour there would still be plenty of time to win the match. The Arab only waited 10 minutes or so before starting the return journey, the jockey not even dismounting. When the Englishman started in pursuit he had to ride hard for 40 miles to catch the Arab who was still stretching along in a comfortable canter; but by the time he came up his horse was beaten and the Arab came in alone.

We are afraid to mention the time as memory may not serve us, but the performance was a good one. The English horse remained in Egypt for several years afterwards winning everything, the races being all of five miles, in fact it was the impossibility of getting anything to beat him, we believe, that caused Ismail Pash to give up the Abasseeyeh Races.

The earliest records

Horse racing began in the Middle East. According to Lady Wentworth, who did a vast amount of research for her book *Thoroughbred Racing Stock and its Ancestors*, there were racing competitions with both hunting and war chariots drawn by two horses. The first of these are seen in Egyptian monuments of around 2500 B.C. She says that racing was in full swing among the Hittites in 1360 B.C., and that the Hittite Treatise of Kikkuli gave minute instructions for training much resembling our own methods. Considerably later Assyrian lion hunts of 800–750 B.C. show a kind of galloping chariot drawn by horses of Arabian type. Horse racing is mentioned in Homer's *Iliad* and the description of the horses used suggests the Arabian type, quite different from those of the Parthenon.

Lady Wentworth, in *The World's Best Horse*, says that in the first races to be run in Arabia horses were kept thirsty and trained to race loose to the nearest water. She cites a celebrated pre-Islamic race of Dahes and El Ghabra in which Quays 'was tricked' into matching his horses against those of Hutheyfa over 14 miles for a stake of 100 camels.

There was racing in the Kingdom of Hira in A.D. 120 and King Bahram had a large collection of horses and used to test them by racing. The Prophet Mohammed conducted Arab racing in Syria from A.D. 624–687; he had a great admiration for the Arabian and, according to Lady Wentworth, 'wrote reams in its praise'.

The Middle East

Arabian horses have raced in Egypt, Syria and Persia for at least a thousand years. In the thirteenth century Sultan El Naseri established an exceptional stud, collecting Arabians from many of the best horse-breeding tribes and paying high prices for some of them – he is said to have given 64,000 Turkish pounds for the racing El Karta filly. The Sultan built hippodromes and race-tracks and at Kabak there were yearly races with all the princes present.

Six hundred years later a famous collection of Arabians was made by Mohammed Ali, Viceroy of Egypt, who also purchased horses of the highest quality. He was succeeded by his grandson, Abbas Pasha I, who added to the stud. After his death in 1854 many of the horses were sold. One of the principal buyers was Ali Pasha Sherif who carried on the stud in Egypt until 1896. One of his finest stallions was Wazir, a grey Seglawi Jedran of Ibn Sudan, who was unbeaten at all distances and lived to be nearly 30 years of age.

Wilfrid and Lady Anne Blunt raced Mesaoud, purchased as a colt from the stud of Ali Pasha Sherif, in Cairo in 1891. Mesaoud was imported to England later that year and became a famous sire – his name probably appears more frequently in the pedigrees of horses around the world than any other Arabian stallion.

Egypt was one of the most important countries for racing during the early part of the present century and many studs concentrated on breeding solely for racing. H. E. Fouad Abaza explained how in 1908 the Royal Agricultural Society of Egypt was using Thoroughbred stallions in an endeavour 'to improve and put vigour into the progeny of the little local mares'. The experiment was not successful, however, as it became apparent that the half-breds were of poor conformation and inclined to be vicious, so were not popular. In 1914 the Society decided to change its policy and the Thoroughbreds were replaced with Arabians of high quality.

Baghdad was a prominent centre for racing and for buying and selling racehorses, and a report written in 1935 says that 75 meetings were held each year. The track was one and a quarter miles round and the going consisted of a slight layer of sand on a cement-like foundation. It was remarked that nothing but Arab horses – which ran unshod – could stand such a test. About 1,000 horses trained 'privately' took part, ridden by well-turned-out native jockeys.

At around the same time racing took place in what was then Palestine. Some of the horses taking part were locally bred and there were doubts as to whether they were pure Arabians. There were also horses brought in from Syria and Trans-Jordan and some of the stock bred in the Gaza–Beersheba district (the main horse-breeding area) were sent to Egypt for racing.

Dr Ahmed Mabrouk, describing in 1938 a journey he had recently undertaken to Arabia when searching for high quality Arabians for the Royal Agricultural Society of Egypt, mentions King Abdel Aziz Seoud holding race meetings in Riyadh every Friday afternoon. Prince Feisul held races in At Ta'if but the comment made was that 'the ugly mares are generally the winners'.

India

The earliest mention of Arabian horses in India was made by Marco Polo, writing about 1290. He mentions the port of 'Kayal', on the coast of Madras, as being 'the city where ships arrive from the Persian Gulf and from Aden and all Arabia laden with horses and with other things for sale'. In 1350 Sultan Alla-Ud-Din was said to have distributed 500 Arab horses as gifts on his son's marriage.

For several hundred years there was a strong trade in importations of Eastern horses into India by way of the Persian Gulf and this continued into the twentieth century. At the outbreak of the First World War in 1914 many Indian cavalry regiments contained a fair proportion of them.

At the time of the arrival of the British in India the Arabian, in addition to its value as a stud horse for improving local stock and for military purposes, was used for sport such as polo, pigsticking and particularly for racing. One of the principal races, the Calcutta Derby, was instituted in 1842 for Arab horses only.

In 1936 Brigadier Anderson (then Secretary of the Arab Horse Society) wrote that it was the demand of the racecourse alone which kept alive the importation of Arabian horses into India, 700 to 800 being imported annually from ports in the Persian Gulf.

The chief centres for racing were Bombay, Madras and Poona; Arab races were also run by the Ceylon Turf Club and at the lesser race meetings in India. The stakes were high and fields so large that it was frequently necessary to divide races.

The races were also used as tests prior to selecting the highest quality specimens to go as sires to the Government stud and breeding centres, the additional test of the racecourse being considered a sure indication of soundness, stamina and courage. Brigadier Anderson mentions that at Bombay and Poona it was common to see Arabians racing in the top class and at the top weights at an age when most of their Thoroughbred confrères had long since retired from the track. He adds that it was remarkable to observe with what consistency the Arabians would come out week after week to race throughout the season.

Mention has already been made in an earlier chapter of the stallion Maidan, who had an excellent record in India; there were many more. Mundil and Khundil raced up to the age of 15 and were still high up in top-class handicaps when retired to stud. The bay Singer was the winner of ten races between a mile and one and three-quarter miles including the Governor's Cup. Purity, a chestnut, raced from seven furlongs to one and three-quarter miles, and won six races including the Governor's Cup twice.

The grey Silver Thrush was outstanding, both in beauty and quality, and he was a great racehorse. His fame was such that an enthusiastic American breeder sent the Thoroughbred mare Ampeline (Pomme de Terre ex Ampelete) all the way from England to India to be covered by him. The mare returned to Newmarket where she produced a filly, and both went later to America. It is interesting to note all these stallions were under 15 hands.

Early racing in England

Lady Wentworth asserts that the first racehorses recorded by name in England were Arundel, an imported Arabian stallion owned by Sir Bevys of Hamptown, and the Arabian mare Truncefice who came over from Bradmond, King of Damascus. They raced over a seven-mile course at the Court of King Edgar, in London, in 957 A.D. Arundel won but the mare 'Swiftest Truncefice' was celebrated in verse 600 years later as a proverbially renowned example of a brood mare.

Over the centuries there were of course many other Eastern horses imported into England and raced. Elizabeth I kept a number in racing stables at Greenwich. James I built stables at Newmarket and his racehorses carried much Oriental blood. Cromwell made efforts to purchase through the Levant Company and many prominent persons owned and raced Oriental horses.

The value of the Arabian as the progenitor of modern racehorses has never been in doubt but it is of interest to read the words of Osmer (quoted by Lady Wentworth in *The World's Best Horse*), a noted veterinary surgeon who knew the Godolphin Arabian well, written in 1761:

Arabian horses and their descendants when properly chosen are preferable to all others whether you are to be carried a mile or a thousand, let the weight be what it will, nor have other horses such true courage or calmness of temper, nor can they bear fatigue with equal fortitude as our severe discipline of training will in some measure help to show . . . Now it has here been allowed that the Arabians are the best kind of horses we know of from whom it can be expected to breed a racer or in other words the most perfect horse. Arabian horses being better constituted for action than other horses do by means hereof excel all others. The sinew of the mountain (desert) Arab is like a bar of iron hence the degree of difference between him and some other Asiatick horses and all other horses of the world. But we understand so little about the matter that these very horses are called weak cat-legged things and our great coarse brutes with hairy legs, thick skins and lax fibres, are considered much the strongest . . . The attachment of some men to what is commonly called 'a good English horse' is as absurd as the objection of sportsmen to blood, i.e. cat-legged things. As to Barbs I mean those only which I have seen, all have a particular cast or turn in their hinder parts from which they may in general be easily known by the observant eye.

The 1884 Arabian races

When Wilfrid and Lady Anne Blunt started their Crabbet Stud in 1878 they had thoughts of stock bred there being of use through giving a fresh infusion of Arabian blood into the Thoroughbred, which Blunt considered was needed. He began talks with the Jockey Club for a race under their rules for Arabians only. After two years of discussion with the three stewards it was eventually agreed to hold one at Newmarket in 1884.

Blunt felt it was essential that the very best racing Arabians should run in this race which was intended to demonstrate that the qualities of the Arabian were still vital to the Thoroughbred. The best in training at that time were in India, where racing was a popular sport with the British community, and he tried to persuade owners to bring over their best horses. In the event only two came, Dictator and Kismet, who was unbeaten in India.

The race was held on 2 July over two miles on the July course. It was a weight for age sweepstake and there were eight runners. The winner was Asil, who beat the favourite Dictator by four lengths, with Rataplan third. According to Lady Anne Blunt there were conflicting reports about the way in which the race was run but the fact was that only Asil had been properly trained. The performance of the horses was not impressive and as a demonstration of the racing ability of the Arabian as compared to Thoroughbreds it was a failure.

A second race was held at Sandown Park on 22 July over a mile and Asil was beaten by a short head, but the following day in another race for Arabians, this time over 5 furlongs, Asil won by four lengths. Despite the Jockey Club being unimpressed by the performance of the Arabians an attempt was made to revive interest the following year. A mixed race for Arabians and Thoroughbreds was held at the second Newmarket Spring meeting on 20 May, but as only two horses ran it resolved into a match between Asil and the Thoroughbred Iambic. Over a distance of three miles it ended in a resounding victory for Iambic, who won by 20 lengths.

It was not until 1923 that a further attempt was made to revive Arab racing. A one-mile race under National Pony Turf Club Rules was held at Bideford, by the Shebbertown Race Club on 6 August. It was won by Belka

(Rijm ex Bereyda) with Shahzada (Mootrub ex Ruth Kesia) second. In 1928 a race for Arabians registered with the Arab Horse Society was held at the Portsmouth races, when the imported stallion Fedaan won from Sainfoin (Rasim ex Safarjal). These two horses dominated the two races which were held at Northolt Park in 1929, where again the stakes were guaranteed by the Pony Turf Club – Fedaan beating Sainfoin in the first, with a reversal of this order in the second race held a month later.

Although Arab racing flourished in the Middle East and in India and Ceylon, and started in Poland prior to the First World War, there was a reluctance on the part of the existing racing authorities in England to provide races for Arabians, and after 1929 half a century was to pass before Arab racing as we know it today began.

Sainfoin, race winner and show champion.

Eastern horses as Thoroughbred foundation stock

The fact that all Thoroughbreds trace in the male line to three Eastern sires is well known. What deserves to be equally well known is the influence that a great many other Oriental stallions and mares had on the founding of the Thoroughbred breed.

The terms 'Eastern' and 'Oriental' are used here to denote all Arabians and those such as Barbs and Turcomans which were imported into England before there was any recognised stud book to record their ancestry.

The General Stud Book (G.S.B.), devoted to the Thoroughbred and considered the world's greatest stud record, was begun in 1791 by James Weatherby with the aim of producing a comprehensive register calculated to reduce the risks of fraud and error in attributing pedigrees. It was called 'General' to differentiate it from the various private herdbooks that had been kept since the previous century by numerous breeders. This first publication, containing a small collection of pedigrees extracted from Racing Calendars and sale papers, was believed by Mr Weatherby to consist of a 'greater mass of authentic information respecting Horses than has ever before been collected together'.

We have seen that Arabian horses had been coming to England for several hundred years before the eighteenth century. From then onwards there are more specific records of Eastern horses brought to England, but often disputes over exact details. Many owners had their best horses painted and in several instances more than one portrait of a named horse was executed by different artists. Small discrepancies in portraying the animal often led to violent controversies over the veracity of a portrait. This coupled with sometimes less than adequate documentation inevitably led to conjecture as to the bona fide credentials of the horse in question and, more often than not, it was the most famous and successful sires which aroused the greatest controversy!

Many of the early horses were known by the name of their owner. Thus we have such as the Leedes Arabian (about 1695), one of the most important male influences in pedigrees, though not in direct sire line. The Alcock Arabian (1704), also known as the Pelham or Ancaster Arabian (he was the property of the Duke of Ancaster from 1722–4), was a grey, and his colour has been handed down unbroken for over a score of generations; one of his most famous descendants was Mumtaz Mahal, the then Aga Khan's 'flying filly'.

The Leedes Arabian.

So much has been written about the three foundation sires, the Darley Arabian, the Godolphin Arabian, and the Byerley Turk, that only a brief history will be given here.

First to come to England was the Byerley Turk in 1688. He was owned by Captain Robert Byerley who had acquired the horse as a spoil of war when he was fighting against the Turks in Hungary. Captain Byerley used him as a charger. He became known as 'Byerley's Treasure' and was said to be the envy of brother officers. Later the stallion was retired to stud at his owner's home, Goldsborough Hall.

The Byerley Turk.

The Darley Arabian was purchased by Thomas Darley who, in a letter written in Aleppo dated 21 December 1703 to his brother Richard, said:

Since your father expects I should send him a stallion I esteem myself happy in a colt I bought a year and a half ago . . . his colour bay; and his near foot before with both his hind feet, have white upon them; he has a blaze down his face something of the largest; he is about 15 hands high; of the most esteemed race amongst the Arabs both by sire and dam, and the name of the race is called Manicha.

The Darley Arabian.

The Godolphin Arabian, or Sham as he was known, was purchased by Edward Coke of Derbyshire in 1730. Mr Coke, who died in 1733, had bequeathed mares to the Earl of Godolphin, who then bought Sham from Roger Williams, who had inherited Mr Coke's stallions. Sham had been one of four Arabians presented to the King of France in 1730. He was described by Vicomte de Manty, who saw him in France, as being:

> of beautiful conformation, exquisitely proportioned with large hocks, well let down, with legs of iron, with unequalled lightness of forehand – a horse of incomparable beauty whose only flaw was being headstrong. An essentially strong stallion type, his quarters broad in spite of being half starved, tail carried in true Arabian style.

Bruce Lowe, an Australian, has traced every Thoroughbred back on the distaff side to one of 43 foundation mares, which he numbered according to the number of wins in classic races accumulated by their descendants. Lady Wentworth disputed his number of mares and says it should be 18, as she found that the rest trace back to those already allocated a number. Though conceding that the system of numbering is interesting, Lady Wentworth, who had inherited from her mother the mathematical bent of her grandmother Ada (daughter of Lord Byron), a brilliant mathematician who helped Charles Babbage develop his 'difference engine' (a prototype of the

The Godolphin Arabian.

modern computer), considered it an unsound breeding guide as she reckoned a pedigree of 26 generations represents 134, 217, 726 units. At the time she was writing (1938) pedigrees were nearly 29 generations which would make the total 536, 870, 912 units. This meant that one mare on the bottom line (tail female) represents only 29 to 53, 670, 883 against her. Lady Wentworth points out that the influence of the mare would be quite negligible unless continually repeated, and gives as an example the mare No. 6, Old Bald Peg (an Arabian, she maintains), who swamps the pedigrees even when not in the bottom line. She quoted Sir Theodore Cook, who wrote: 'It is impossible to label certain sires and dams with various figures, treat them like multiplication tables and sit down and wait for the result.' Lady Wentworth, who had an uncanny flair for predicting crosses that would 'nick' well and who was aware too of imponderables,

A 'Royal Mare' of Charles II, c. 1685. (J. Sartorius, Senior)

wisely states that breeders should 'use common sense and not rely too much on mathematics, however fascinating'.

According to Lady Wentworth, all Thoroughbreds trace back in the female line to about 25 to 30 mares. She commented that modern pedigrees concentrate more and more on about a score of these original 'tap roots'. The fact that over 7,000 brood mares and their progeny recorded in the G.S.B. at that time trace to 'so small a number of mares in the female line is no less of a phenomenon than their descent from three ancestors in the male line'. This aspect of breeding is borne out in the stud books of Arabians too. As lines of both sires and dams die out after many generations of selective breeding, it will often be found that pedigrees trace back to a very small genetic base.

As has been said, many of the original mares were of Oriental blood. In addition to Old Bald Peg, others include Tregonwell's Natural Arabian Mare, Burton's Natural Barb Mare, and Darcy's Layton Violet Grey Arabian Mare. Others were sired by Eastern horses or had Oriental blood in their pedigrees from earlier imports. The 'Royal Mares', from which many of the 'original' progenitors are descended, trace back to mares imported from the Levant by Charles II, a monarch with an exceptional eye for beauty.

*A Hampton Court
'Royal Mare' of Charles II.
(J. Sartorius, Senior)*

*'Blood Royal, an Arab of the
Purest Caste. From the Imaun
of Muscat to William IV.
Purchased by P. D. P.
Duncombe at the Royal Stud
Sale, Hampton Court, 1837.'
(Robert Morley, signed and
dated 1838)*

Although it cannot be claimed that the Thoroughbred is of pure Oriental origin, there was a great deal of close in-breeding to the best-known stallions and mares in the early days of the foundation of the breed, which obviously further intensified the preponderance of Eastern blood.

CHAPTER FOUR

Modern Arab racing around the world

Great Britain

The concept of racing Arabian horses in Britain today was formulated by a few enthusiastic people who believed that it would benefit the breed if it could be demonstrated as being highly capable of standing up to the rigours of racing. It was hoped too that exposure on the turf would help to counteract the considerable prejudice against the Arabian amongst those horsemen who saw it merely as a show butterfly. In addition, racing could become an enjoyable sport for members of the Arab Horse Society, and provide useful occupation for many talented and energetic horses. The idea was put to the A.H.S., and it was duly agreed to hold two trial meetings.

The first took place on 10 July 1978 at Hawthorn Hill, a disused racecourse in Berkshire, and the second at Larkhill, the military point-to-point course near Salisbury, on 14 August. Thirty-one runners took part in six races at Hawthorn Hill with an assorted collection of 'jockeys' and much enthusiasm from all concerned. Who could have guessed on that day how far the sport would have progressed by 1996 – perhaps too much and too quickly in some respects.

There can be little true comparison with Arab racing in other European countries. For one thing, in Britain it is run as an amateur sport; consequently horses, owners and trainers participating far outnumber those of other countries. There are many more race meetings in Britain and they are solely for Arabians, Anglo-Arabs and part-breds, instead of the inclusion of races specifically for Arabians in fixtures otherwise devoted to Thoroughbreds, as is the common practice on the Continent.

From the beginning the Arab Horse Society wished to have the permission of the Jockey Club (the ruling body for British Thoroughbred racing) as authentication of their new venture. Despite the very modest beginnings the Jockey Club was sufficiently impressed by the professional approach of the organisation to give their approval for the continuance of the sport. Four meetings were held in 1979, and weights were fixed at 10 stone for pure-breds of four and five years old (no horse under the age of four is allowed to race) over six furlongs, and 11 stone for those of six and over, with distances from six furlongs to two and a half miles. Anglos and part-breds were to carry 11 stone with races of one and a quarter miles.

By 1981 the number of A.H.S. members participating warranted a fixture of five meetings and the Jockey Club gave their approval for on-course bookmakers. A further advance came the following year when a licensed course was used for the first time; also it was decided to introduce grades to differentiate maidens from those who had won.

Arab racing is run entirely by the A.H.S. under the jurisdiction of the Jockey Club. A Race Committee in charge of organisation reports to the Council of the Society, and the office work is done at the Society's headquarters. It is, however, completely dependent on voluntary helpers for stewarding and many of the other tasks concerning the practical side of running each race meeting. Without this voluntary help, generously given by so many, Arab racing could never have been possible. Up to 1983 it had not been a financially viable enterprise, but that year saw a small profit from the five successful meetings.

Start of the 1995 racing season at Taunton.

A further advance came the following year when a generous donation from Sheikh Hamdan Bin Rashid Al Maktoum enabled the Society to hold a meeting at Kempton Park, a grade one racecourse. The principal race was the Dubai Stakes, and it was won by Valina (Al Nahr Montino ex Radsilla). In 1985 the first International meeting was held at Kempton Park with two races on the card for entries from overseas. Horses came from France, Germany, the Netherlands, Norway and Spain, with the French taking both races with Cherifa and Benji, full sister and brother by Cheri Bibi out of Managhi. In 1990 a second International meeting was held at Windsor, sponsored by Sheikh Zayed Bin Sultan Al Nahayan, President of the United Arab Emirates. This meeting was switched to Kempton Park the following year, and it too has become an annual event. Qualifying races are run during the season for the Championships held at Goodwood in October, when the prestigious races for the Champion Sprinter (6 furlongs), Long Distance (2½ miles), Mare and Juvenile (4 years) are held as a grand finale to the season.

The sport grew steadily, the number of horses doubling between 1983 and

43

1985 when there was a total of 179 in training; there were 150 owners, 123 trainers and 141 jockeys registered with the Society.

Entries had risen to embarrassing numbers by 1987, one race at Huntingdon having 102 aspirants! Balloting had to be introduced, but grade 3 horses were allowed one priority card (for use in grade 3 races only) each per season, which when used guaranteed they would be accepted for that one race. Races were also divided where this was possible. There was an obvious need to enlarge and in 1988, with over 400 horses registered for racing, 15 meetings were held. Figures show that Arab racing for A.H.S. members reached a peak in 1989 when there were 433 owners, 260 trainers, 282 jockeys and 504 horses in training, although the number of meetings remained at 15. Six more were added in 1990, which meant that there was an Arab race meeting somewhere in England nearly every week from May until early October.

It was about this time that horses began to be imported with the prime intention of racing them. First on the scene in 1989 were a number from Russia – 22 were registered for Arab racing in 1990. But the huge influx of foreign-bred Arabians came in 1993, mostly from France and the U.S.A. By then a number of Arab sheikhs were buying and the first auction by Tattersalls of Arabian racehorses was held at Newmarket. Of the 42 offered 13 sold; top price of 62,000 guineas was paid by Sheikh Hamdan Al Maktoum for the Russian stallion Normative (Mascat ex Narta), which later won the first race for Arabians to be held this century at a Thoroughbred meeting, another innovation of that year.

In 1994, 23 race meetings were held, 410 Arabians and 49 Anglo-Arabs were registered in training, and 175 trainers were registered. Part-breds, which were dropped from racing in 1988, are once again eligible to race provided they are blood-typed and comply with registration requirements.

The importation of so many proven Arabian racehorses, most of which joined the larger trainers, brought a change in the racing scene. There has been a decline in the overall number of owners, trainers and jockeys and there are now some owners with quite a number of horses and a few trainers with large yards; but the vast majority of British owners have only one or two horses in training, and there are still some who own, train and even ride their own horses. A situation has developed where the small owners and trainers – many of whom are the 'original' backbone and dedicated instigators of the sport – feel they are being pushed out through insufficient recognition of the truth that 'little is good'. Their concern was highlighted and brought into the open in 1994, when the Council of the A.H.S. approved a Race Committee proposal to come into force in 1995 allowing professional jockeys to ride in international races. A large number of racing members were against this move and at an Open Forum in 1995, chaired by the President, the Society was urged to consider in greater depth all implications relevant to the future development of Arab racing in the U.K.

Successful racehorses

Many of the successful Arabians racing in the U.K. have remained in training for several years, a tribute to their trainers and confirmation of their soundness and courage, as well as their ability. In this résumé it is only possible to mention a few of them.

Amongst those winning during the early years was Shadow Royal (Royal Drift ex Bright Dawn) who in fact won the one and a half mile race at the very first meeting at Hawthorn Hill. He ran for six seasons and in his 14 races over distances from six furlongs to one and three-quarter miles he had 10 wins, 3 seconds and a fourth; in those days horses of six years and over carried 11 stone. In 1980, during his racing career, he also came fourth in the A.H.S. Ride and Tie. Shadow Royal had competed in endurance before he raced, winning a Golden Horseshoe in 1977 when six years old. After winning the Long Distance Race Championship for the second time he was retired from racing and continued in endurance up to the age of 16.

In the first season or two of racing a horse would sometimes run twice at a meeting. Mazatir (Manalix ex Zarah of Knotting) in 1979 won over six furlongs and then came out again to win over one mile six furlongs. He too raced for five seasons and accumulated 11 wins, 6 seconds and 4 thirds. Rippling Amber (Cochise ex Rippling Blue) was another to score twice at the same meeting when he won the five furlong and the seven furlong races at Larkhill in 1982; in his four seasons of racing he had five wins.

In the early days of the sport many horses started racing at a much more advanced age than is now the case, and sometimes after competing in another discipline. Shomran (Sidi Bou Sbeyel ex Halima) was an outstanding example of the versatile racehorse. He had won in the show-ring

Shadow Royal, ridden by J. Elliot, led in by his breeder, D. T. Hulme, after winning at Larkhill.

in-hand and under saddle and was a B.S.J.A. registered show-jumper in Senior and Junior categories before he began racing in 1986 at the age of 11. The little 14.1½ hh bay stallion was ridden by 16-year-old Annette Harrison and they won five races 'off the reel'. Shomran set two records; at Worcester in 1987 he became the U.K. six furlong record holder in 1 minute 17 seconds; the same year he was fourth at Evry in France, the first British-bred horse to be placed abroad. Both records held at the time of his death in 1993. Shomran had three seasons racing and won nine times; in his last season at the age of 14 he had a win and a second and was only unplaced once when he was fifth at Kempton, having suffered injury at the start. He was hunted most winters and aged 17 he appeared at the A.H.S. show at Malvern in the show-jumping and flew round to take the third prize. Happily this star performer has left numerous progeny.

Two horses who rivalled each other in the early 1980s were Magic Knight (Sir Lancelot ex Magic Flare) and Mishlah (Silver Flame ex Silver Mantle). Both made their debut in 1983 and were in the Top Ten for that year. Over five seasons of racing Mishlah had four wins, five seconds and five thirds.

Magic Knight went on to become one of the most consistent racehorses ever seen in the U.K. He raced for six years and in 41 starts he had 13 wins, 9 seconds and 9 thirds. In 1984 he won the Warwick Stakes over six furlongs at the Kempton International meeting and in the following four years, when this race was opened to horses from abroad and became known as the Dunhill Champion Stakes (now the Zabeel Stakes), he was fourth and best British-bred in 1985 and 1988, second in 1986 to the French-bred Djamel, and third in 1987. He also was ridden by a young jockey, for Alison Webster (as she was then) was only 16 when he started racing.

In 1985 Carabineer (Carbine ex Cinders) began his racing career at the age of 11 and, winning five of his six races, including the Laybrook Stakes over two miles one furlong at Goodwood by 20 lengths, he was the Leading Racehorse for that year. In 1986 he won the top international race at Kempton Park, the Dubai Stakes over one and a half miles, beating the French mare Cherifa. Carabineer went on to win a further seven races over distances of one to two miles in the next three seasons.

The following year another British-bred horse triumphed in the Dubai Stakes, the five-year-old Ashmahl (Ahmoun ex Koralina), again with a French mare, Margau (Manganate ex Mandore), in second place. With five wins in 1987 Ashmahl was the Leading Racehorse of the Year. He continued racing for three more seasons and then reappeared in 1993 at the age of 11 to win three times. Also in 1987 Ibn Alkhalif (Count Hazariee ex Countess Cara) won the Dunhill World Championship Sprint and three other races.

In 1988 Seheran (Silver Flame ex Shottifa) emerged in his fourth season as one of the best long distance horses to be bred in the U.K. From seven starts he had six wins, culminating in taking the two mile five furlong Laybrook Stakes at Goodwood by nine lengths, despite a stirrup leather having broken over a mile from home!

From 1988 to 1990 the award for the Leading Horse went to Anglo-Arabs – with one exception when the Leading Mare in 1990 was Duma. However, there has never been a large number of Anglo-Arabs racing compared to Arabians and there has been a tendency for one or two to dominate each season and therefore accumulate more wins.

ABOVE LEFT *Carabineer and Miss K. R. Bradley after winning the Dubai Stakes at Kempton Park in 1986.*

ABOVE RIGHT *Ashmahl, ridden by Miss S. M. Wilkinson winning the Cambridge Stakes at Huntingdon in 1987.*

LEFT *P. Middleton and Seheran, winner of the Hambleton Stakes at Thirsk in 1988, going down to the start.*

In the early days of racing El Trapero (Arctic Prince ex Ona Dollar) was one of the best Anglos. He ran his first race in 1980 and his last in 1986. In all he won 15 races and in 1984, when 12 years old, he was unbeaten in his five starts, all over one and a quarter miles. He also hunted for seven seasons.

In 1983 two very good Anglos made their debut as four year olds, Woodlands Court Magician (Sir Magic ex Stormy Trial) and Suntal Golden Token (Dundrum St George ex Sheila's Token). In six seasons Suntal Golden Token, who raced over distances of one and a quarter miles and over, had 19 wins, 3 seconds and 2 thirds.

Woodlands Court Magician was a sprinter and although not such a prolific winner – 10 wins, 21 seconds and 4 thirds – he achieved a remarkable record in the Anglo-Arab sprint at the Kempton International meetings. There is a tradition at Kempton Park that if any horse wins the same race at the course three times his achievement is marked by having a saddling-up stable named after it. By winning the Raynham Stakes for the third consecutive year in 1986 Woodlands Court Magician was honoured in this way. He won a fourth time in 1987, beating Edmund Dante whose remarkable career began the previous season.

Edmund Dante was by Freddie Darling out of Treasure Chest and was of only six and a quarter per cent Arab blood. It was not until 1991 that the ruling was changed so that to qualify for racing Anglo-Arabs had to have a minimum of twelve and a half per cent Arab blood. In the five seasons that he raced Edmund Dante amassed 24 wins, 45 seconds and 3 thirds.

With 27 wins from 38 starts Just Jet (Sibec ex Invisible Justice) has been outstanding since 1989, mostly over distances from one and a quarter to one and a half miles. He was Leading Four and Five-year-old Racehorse in 1989 and 1990, missed a season in 1993 due to a leg injury, but in 1994 won four times, including the Anglo-Arab Championship at Goodwood. Just Jet beat the record for the most races won in British Arab racing when he gained his twenty-fifth victory at Uttoxeter in 1995. He won the Anglo Sprint Championship and also the Mile Championship, which was run at the first Arab race meeting to be held at Newmarket, and was rated Leading Anglo-Arab of the Year.

Two mares whose Anglo-Arab progeny have made a name for themselves are Royal Regalia and Scottish Fable. Royal Regalia's outstanding foals are the two full sisters by Imperial Majesty. Kelway Royal Princess was the Leading Race Mare in 1989 with four wins, three seconds and a third. The brilliant Kelway Crystal Light was the Leading Mare in 1991 and created a record by being unbeaten in her eight races that year. She continued to dominate the scene and was Leading Anglo-Arab in 1993 and started the

1994 season with two wins, but unfortunately a severe injury racing resulted in her retirement for the rest of the season.

Scottish Fable has been ably represented by two sons, Scottish Legend, by Hopton Lane, and Scottish Express by Pony Express. Scottish Legend competed mostly in long distance races and won the Colin Pearson Championship Stakes over two and a half miles at Goodwood in 1991, with his half-brother in third place. 1992 was Scottish Express's year – with nine wins to his credit, including the Hatta Stakes at the Kempton International meeting and the Championship at Goodwood, he was the Leading Anglo-Arab Racehorse of the year.

A pure-bred mare with a particularly interesting career is Miralda (Kasadi ex Mariamne). Having produced her first foal at the age of four in 1986 she then raced for three years, in 1987 winning over six furlongs and coming second to Ashgate Comet at the Kempton Park International, and the following year coming second in the James Capel Mare Championship. Miralda had a year off to produce her second foal in 1990 and then returned to racing for another two seasons. She won again and had three more seconds and a third, ending her career at the age of ten with a very game second to the American-bred Elite Star Ku (Tikis Flaming Star ex Tikis Ellice) and beating by a head the British-bred Silvena in the Qatar Mares Championship at Goodwood. Miralda's record in this Championship was two seconds, a third and a fourth; in addition she proved that it is possible for mares to alternate the role of brood mare and racehorse.

Razeldah (Ragos ex Joan El Dahab), who beat Miralda in the 1988 Mare

ABOVE LEFT *Just Jet, ridden by Sarah Kelleway, winning the Imperial Mile at Kempton in 1990.*

ABOVE RIGHT *Kelway Crystal Light ten lengths clear as she wins the Malvern Stakes at Worcester in 1991, ridden by Mrs R. A. Bursua.*

Miralda, ridden by R. Norman (right), winning the Stowe Stakes at Towcester in 1991 from Ibn Nawarb (Nawarb ex Princess of Sakkara).

Championship, emphasised this point because she too produced a foal in the middle of her racing career. Razeldah was successful over longer distances as well as sprinting and won four times, with three seconds and one third.

Silvena (Klarnet ex Silvretta Sky) began her career in 1990 and soon established herself as an outstanding racehorse. She had 11 wins and 6 thirds over six furlongs and a mile in three seasons before being retired to stud.

The Russian-bred mare, Diskoteka (Strij ex Nasechka), notched up eight wins and a third in three seasons from 1989. However, undoubtedly one of the best Russian horses was Duma (Naftalin ex Mechta) who in four seasons from 1989 had 12 wins, 3 seconds and a third. She was the Leading Mare of 1990 when her wins included the Abu Dhabi International Oaks at Windsor over one and a half miles, the Mare Championship at Kempton and the Dunhill Sprint Championship at Goodwood. In 1991 she won the Dubai Stakes, beating Drug (Prizrak ex Karinka) and Roumba du Cassou

Duma, ridden by Mrs D. J. Camp-Simpson, at Windsor in 1990 where she won the Abu Dhabi International Oaks.

(Baroud III ex Java), and the Sprint Championship again, and the next year she won the Deira Stakes at the Kempton Dubai meeting. Duma also has the distinction of being the first British-trained Arabian to win an international race abroad – in 1992 she beat the Dubai Stakes winner, Djouribi (Cheri Bibi ex Djouranta), and the American-bred Way to Go in France's second most important race, the one mile three furlong Trophée International du Cheval.

Ashgate Comet, by Sky Crusader (who for several years was the Leading Sire in Arab racing) out of La Maja Majala, had his first win as a four year old at the 1987 Kempton International meeting over five furlongs. He was the leading pure-bred racehorse in 1991 and in all had 12 wins, 6 seconds and 5 thirds up to 1994, in which year he came third at Huntingdon at the age of 11.

Another horse demonstrating that age is no bar to winning is Balaton's Gem (Balaton ex Nasa) who won his first race in 1989 at the age of nine, and who was still winning in 1994. Most of his races were in distances of one and a half to two and a half miles, and over six seasons he had 8 wins, 9 seconds and 17 thirds. Two of his best races were the 1990 Dubai Stakes, when he came second to the French-bred Roumba du Cassou, and third in the Al Ain International Derby at the U.A.E. Kempton meeting in 1992 behind another French horse, Atus de Domenjoi (Cheri Bibi ex Sbah Hani), and Inyalah. When 14 years old Balaton's Gem came third in the two mile race at the 1994 Kempton U.A.E. meeting.

D'Just Casey (King Cotton Gold ex Djewizza) was just one year older when he won a Qatar Sprint Qualifier in 1994 by five lengths. He started racing in 1990; earlier victories of note include the Jumeirah Stakes over a mile at the 1992 Kempton International and the Tarif Stakes at Kempton U.A.E. meeting in 1993 in a new pure-bred course record time.

Inyalah (Kais ex Ikbal) at seven years old had an excellent season in 1992 with three wins and four seconds, which included the Dubai Stakes where he divided two French horses, Djouribi and Danzine (Zulus ex Dandoura), as well as his second in the Al Ain Derby. That same year saw the closely related Irus, by Kais out of Ino, a daughter of Ikbal, make his debut with three wins, a second and a third. His wins included the Tarif Stakes at Kempton, in which he was second the following year. In 1995, in his fourth year of racing, Irus had the best season of his career at the age of seven. Not only did he make history when winning the first Arab race to be run at Epsom over the Derby course, he won six of his eleven starts, ending the season by taking the Long Distance Championship over two and a half miles at Goodwood. Irus was rated Leading Pure-bred Racehorse of the Year, over the previous winner, Vert Olive.

Momentz (Seattle ex Mishanif) was in his fourth season in 1994 and eight years old. He won the Sprint Championship at Goodwood in 1992 and 1993 and had three wins in 1994.

Aflame (Silver Halo ex Darjella) won his first two races in 1990 when six years old. Three wins at distances of six furlongs to one mile followed (with one win over two miles) and in 1993 he took the title of Top Pure-bred Racehorse, established by a points system, when he had three wins, two seconds and two thirds. He also began to establish a reputation for being one of the best British-bred horses to take on the imports.

In 1993 Aflame was second to the Russian-bred Normative in the first Arabian race to be held on a Thoroughbred card. At the age of ten in the 1994 races at Thoroughbred meetings he was beaten by a short head by French-bred Vert Olive (Elbing ex Bise du Moulon), six years his junior, at Lingfield – Vert Olive went on to be Top Pure-bred in 1994 – and second again to him at Brighton. Another French horse, Virgule al Maury (Kesberoy ex Valse du Cassou) was in third place, a reversal of their position in both the Zaabeel Stakes at the Dubai International and the Al Wathba Stakes at the U.A.E. Emirates Day at Kempton Park. Finally Aflame was third to the French-bred Souman D'Aroco (Manganate ex Soumeria) and Normative at the Kempton race on the Thoroughbred card; in addition he had two wins, a second and two thirds at A.H.S. meetings.

Despite the successes of all these horses it was the brilliant Bengali D'Albret (Cheri Bibi ex Mangalie D'Albret) who was the outstanding

ABOVE *Aflame, ridden by P. Winks, beating Barabinsk (Strij ex Barhatnaja) in the Raynham Stakes at Market Rasen, 1994.*

Leading racehorse in the U.K. in 1994 with five wins, the French-bred Vert Olive.

Bengali D'Albret winning the Dubai Stakes at Kempton Park, 1994, ridden by S. Walker.

French-bred horse of 1994, not only in the U.K. but on the Continent as well. He created records by winning the Dubai Stakes at Kempton for a second consecutive year, and also had successive wins in the Al Ain Derby at the Kempton U.A.E. meeting and in France at the Coupe D'Europe at Evry. Bengali D'Albret made his final racecourse appearance in an Arab race on a Thoroughbred card at Nottingham in July 1995. Earlier in the season he had won at Huntingdon but was beaten in the Dubai Stakes by the Abu Dhabi trained Darike (Dormane ex Malika Fontenay), who also won the French Derby and the Coupe d'Europe at Evry. After finishing third at Nottingham, Bengali d'Albret was retired at the age of six; he had won 16 of his 23 races.

It can be seen that, although the best of the British-bred Arabians are capable of holding their own against imported horses, over the last two or three years the French Arab racehorses have tended to dominate. Since they have been bred for speed alone this is hardly surprising; but thoughtful breeders, mindful of the need to preserve all the unique characteristics of the Arabian, question this policy, for to breed for one quality alone can eventually unbalance that rare combination which at its best can make so distinguished a horse.

The A.H.S. Marathon

In 1974 the Arab Horse Society inaugurated the Marathon Race over the Olympic distance of 26¼ miles and it has been held nearly every year since then. It is acknowledged to be one of the toughest tests of endurance, courage and fitness of both horse and rider, and is held under strict veterinary supervision which in 1995 was further tightened by the inclusion of one vet check, similar to those of endurance rides.

Although the Marathon is open to other breeds, owners must be members of the A.H.S. Since its inception the race has been dominated by pure-bred, Anglo-Arab and part-bred Arabians. Many of those which take part in the Marathon have proved themselves in endurance; some racehorses have competed with success and others have performed in various disciplines and often been kept fit by cub-hunting, for the event takes place in the autumn and is held in different locations round England.

The 1978 race, over Salisbury Plain, produced one of the closest finishes when only 1.2 seconds separated the first three horses, all of which created a record, with the race run at an overall 18.6 m.p.h. The winner, in 1 hour 24 minutes and 39.8 seconds, was the Anglo-Arab mare Ansty (Armagnac Monarch ex Soracha) who finished 0.4 of a second ahead of the pure-bred gelding Dmitri (General Dorsaz ex Zarka) with another pure-bred, the stallion Dorian (Darjeel ex Orilla), 0.8 seconds behind. Dorian was also a good racehorse, winning races that year at the very first A.H.S. race meeting held at Hawthorn Hill, an achievement he capped with further wins in following years.

The times of winners have, in fact, shown remarkably little variance over the years when run under average weather conditions, considering the different terrain over which the race has been held. Fields have ranged from about a dozen to just over twenty runners.

The little Anglo-Arab stallion Baksheesh won in 1981 and 1983 and was the sire of Shereen, who won in 1985 and came third in 1988. The 1984 winner was the part-bred Pavane, who at the age of 15 was the oldest horse in the race; he came second the following year. Anglo-Arabs dominated in 1987 when the winner was Merelina, a daughter of Ansty.

The previous year, when the race was first run at the Belvoir Castle Estate, it had been the indomitable pure-bred Bonanza who came in first. Bonanza (Banat ex Chantilla) had done just about everything by the time he won the Marathon at the age of ten. He had won in show-jumping, dressage and combined training, hunter trials and one day events. In 1986 he had won a 50 mile endurance race and a three mile race at Newbury, before winning the Marathon.

An Anglo-Arab was the winner in 1988, Malish (Master Spiritus ex Despina), who had been second the year before. The record, which had held for 13 years, was broken in 1992 when the pure-bred Monkton Ramshah (Meagill Giovanni ex Silver Zora) won in 1 hour 15 minutes 1 second. In fact, the first five horses home were within the previous record, although not nearly so close together as in the finish for the 1978 race. It was suggested that the fast times were partly due to the flatness of the Lincolnshire countryside over which the race was run.

The 1993 Marathon had to be cancelled due to bad weather but the record was broken again in 1994. The winner was another pure-bred, Malabar Bolero (Sky Crusader ex Sky Echo), whose time was 1 hour 13 minutes 8 seconds; Monkton Ramshah came in third. The 1995 race, held at Windsor Park, was won by the part-bred endurance horse Univers Du Port (Valsar ex Quenotte Du Medoc), with Granby Ironstone in second place.

Ride and Tie, Cirencester Park, 1979. David and Betsy Borthwick with Claverdon Clubline.

Ride and Tie

The first Ride and Tie took place in the U.S.A. in 1971, the brain-child of Bud Johns, a Vice-President of Levi Strauss. Competition is between teams of two riders/runners and one horse; all teams start together. After travelling a certain distance the mounted rider/runner dismounts, ties his horse and runs on; the runner/rider reaches the horse, mounts and rides, overtaking his partner now running – this process is repeated for the 20 miles of the course, with a minimum of five changes. There are two veterinary checks at which the horse's pulse and respiration rates have to recover to the specified limit before it can continue.

Levi's approached the Arab Horse Society to organise a race in the U.K. in 1979 and Bud Johns backed the organising committee with his help and advice and then acted as starter. The A.H.S. continued to run the event for a number of years.

Europe

Poland

When the Polish Arab Association was founded in 1926 one of the first tasks to be undertaken by its secretary, Dr Edward Skorkowski, was to organise races for Arabians. The object of these races was not to find the fastest horses but to help in the selection of future breeding stock by testing the soundness, endurance and temperament of young Arabians. This last included not only willingness, kind temperament and good sense but in addition the ability to recover quickly from a hard race. While the latter may be to a greater extent physical, the mental attitude of being able to relax and return to normal eating habits quickly after a race is considered equally important. The authorities in charge of the country's state studs felt that it was necessary to ensure that there was no degeneration in any of the qualities of the breed and that performance ability should be assessed as well as type and conformation.

Over nearly 70 years of racing Arabians it has been established in Poland that the best test of their qualities is to take the horses steadily through a programme of lengthening distances, gradually raising the weight carried. The Poles believe that three year olds should run in races of one mile to one and a half miles and four year olds and upwards at distances of one to two miles.

Races for Arabians are integrated with Thoroughbred and half-bred racing on the Warsaw track, where all the horses are now trained. Trainers and jockeys have to have professional licences. Most of the horses come from the national studs and the competition is mainly between the various breeding studs and training stables, though a few are privately owned and trained. The two principal races are the Derby, over one and a half miles and open to both sexes with fillies having a weight allowance, and the Oaks for fillies only over the same distance; in both the minimum age is four. In 1992, 28 races were held for Polish Arabians and there were two international races. The number of horses in training is given as 236, with the Michalow Stud being the most successful as owner and breeder.

Having started regular Arabian racing nearly 70 years ago, despite a break due to the Second World War Poland could well lay claim to exceptional knowledge of successful racing bloodlines. Amongst the earliest horses Koheilan I, bred at Babolna in Hungary in 1922 and known there as Koheilan IV, out of Gazal IV, was a highly successful sire of racehorses and several times held the title of 'Leading Sire of Money Winners', which included three winners of the Derby and three of the Oaks.

Kaszmir (1929 by Farys II ex Hebda) has been described as the greatest

Pamir, by Probat out of Parma, Polish Derby winner and also National Champion Stallion.

racer of his time. He was in training for three years and out of 18 starts over distances from a mile to two miles he won 17 times, including the Derby, and the Criterium three times. His one defeat was coming second to Nemer, a French import, whom he later beat easily.

Wielki Szlem (Ofir ex Elegantka) was a very successful sire of winners. His son Czort, out of Forta, raced for four years and was never out of the first three in 19 races, winning 13 of them, including the Criterium. He raced over all distances and carried 146 pounds in his later runs. Czort was several times the leading sire of money winners.

One of the most remarkable female lines is that of the old Polish mare Szweykowska (foaled 1820). Numerous mares of this line have been great producers of winners, though the family's racing potential was not discovered until over 100 years after the life of the original foundress.

In the early 1990s Email (Palas ex Ejunia), Herb (Wigor ex Heraldyka) and Edyk (Europejczyk ex Depresja) were amongst the most successful racehorses.

Russia

Russian Arabian racing is based on the same principle as that of Poland – it is part of the selection process of future breeding stock. Official racing has taken place since 1950.

In Russia, however, the horses begin racing at an even earlier age than in Poland. The youngstock are broken in during the autumn when they are yearlings and are trotted and cantered; they start racing in about April or May of their two-year-old year.

A description of the system of racing at Tersk, where in 1990 there were 200 horses in training, explains that they are divided between eight trainers, each of whom has a jockey and two assistant jockeys. This ensures good competition as each trainer strives to achieve the best results. The horses are graded into four groups, with corresponding races for each grade; after winning a race they move up to the higher group. Winners of more than three races are tested out in separate groups.

Two year olds are raced every two weeks at distances of 1,000 to 1,800 metres, colts carrying 57 kilos and fillies 55 kilos; three year olds race every 10 to 15 days over 1,600 to 3,200 metres and carry 59 and 56 kilos; four year olds race no more than once weekly at longer distances carrying a kilo more in weight.

They run at the Pyatigorsk, which is a left-handed dirt track, and starting stalls are used. There are main races such as the Summer Prize, and Autumn Prize for fillies (the Oaks) and the Great Pyatigorsk (the Derby) for three year olds. The principal races are usually held at the end of July and four year olds can contest the Elite, the Name of the USSR and the Comparison.

For many years Arabian racehorses from Russia have been sold to other countries in Europe, to the U.S.A., and more recently to the Middle East; and their influence has been considerable. A large number of horses of Russian blood-lines have been bred in the Netherlands, and many of their progeny in turn have also been exported. One Dutch stallion of note is Drug, bred at Tersk, who won the 1991 two and a half mile race at the U.A.E. Kempton Park meeting, and has also won in the show-ring.

After their exportation from Russia many Arabians have continued successfully with their racing career, so achieve mention elsewhere, whilst others retire to stud duties.

Norway and Sweden

In the summer of 1975 the newly formed Norwegian Arab Horse Society invited the Swedish A.H.S. to take part in an 'All Scandinavian Arab Horse Race' on 20 September at Oslo Race Track. Three Swedish owners

Drug, bred at Tersk and domiciled in the Netherlands, winner of the Al Nahiyan International, Kempton Park 1991 and European Show Champion.

sent stallions to make up a field of seven for the 1,600 metre race. The horses were all in good riding condition, though none had been trained especially for racing; they were ridden by English professional jockeys. The winner was the Swedish horse Dofir (Doman ex Moonlight).

At that time Norway had approximately 20 registered pure-bred Arabians, whereas in Sweden there were about 800. The sport grew steadily in Norway where racing continued to take place on the all-weather track Overoll, near Oslo, owned by the Norwegian Jockey Club which controls all racing.

In 1985, 14 races were held for 28 pure-breds, including six from Sweden and one from Denmark. That year the principal event, the N.A.H.F. Trophy Race over 1,600 metres, was won by El Zham (Zareef ex Erobaba). This race is held in conjunction with the Norwegian Arab Horse Society Show.

Enthusiasm for racing in Sweden was fired by the 1975 race at Oslo and a Racing Committee was formed. The Swedish Jockey Club and officials at Stockholm Race Track co-operated and the first official Arab Horse Race in Sweden was held at Taby over 2,000 metres on 1 November 1975. With nine horses aged four and over competing it was won by Caesar (Cedar ex

Samunira), who proved to be one of the best horses running in those early days, winning six out of seven starts.

Eleven races were held at Thoroughbred meetings up to 1976, over distances varying from about six furlongs to one and a quarter miles, with the Swedish Arab Horse Derby and the S.A.F.H. Grand Prix the most prestigious. The rules allowed for Arabians either trained by licensed trainers, or trained at home and brought to the race-track four days before the race and put under the supervision of a professional trainer.

Between 1979 and 1984 Arabian racing flourished in Sweden, with 60 to 70 horses in training and races held on a regular basis at all the race-tracks, but problems arose with racing generally in the country and the organisers put a temporary stop to Arabian racing in 1984.

Now the sport is once again flourishing. The merger of the Arabgalopp Kluben (Arabian Racing Club) with the Central Organisation for Races in Sweden (S.G.C.) encouraged 12 trainers to register 26 horses in training in 1994, and 13 races were held at three tracks and at Blommerod Stud, which set up its own track and holds official Arabian races.

Most of the horses racing in Sweden have come from Poland and one notable stallion is Etman (Gil ex Etruria). He began his racing career in Poland but on being sold to Sweden was shown and became the National

Etman (Gil ex Probat) and Dart (Elart ex Dana) in Sweden.

Champion in 1992. On returning to racing in 1994 he had three wins, two seconds and one third, an admirable achievement and yet further proof that show-ring success and racing prowess are possible in the same horse.

Germany

A racing club for pure-breds, D.R.A.V., was founded in 1976. An encouraging start was made with a small group of about 20 breeders who had 30 horses in training, and 12 races were held in 1979.

Up to 1994 over 200 races for Arabians were run on small category 'B' racetracks; the authorities overseeing Thoroughbred racing would not allow Arab racing on the large category 'A' tracks. Since then the situation has improved and Arab racing has congregated in the north of Germany where all but one of the seven racecourses used are situated. The ten trainers (most of whom are owner-trainers) registered in 1994 are also in the north and between them trained 25 horses for 11 races held. The most successful racing stallion that year was Marbil (Arbil ex Malwina), with two wins and two seconds. Winda (Wingolf I ex Welfin) was the top mare, winning two races and coming third in two more, whilst another horse by Wingolf, Windor out of Negana, won the major race of the season held in Gotha over a distance of 2,200 metres.

Austria

Those responsible for racing acted with both wisdom and efficiency over the manner in which they launched this new activity for Arabians in Austria.

Each year from 1986 to 1989 a race open to Arabians from outside the country, as well as Austrian-owned horses, had been held at Freudenau, on the outskirts of Vienna, Austria's only 'A' track. After it had been won on each occasion by proven racehorses from other countries it was realised that this result was not very encouraging to Austrian breeders. Discussions took place on the advisability of installing races more on the lines of performance testing and for Austrian-owned Arabians only, and after lengthy negotiations with the racecourse management it was decided that the rules of the Austrian Jockey Club should be applied.

In April 1993 the Arabian Racing Club Austria (A.R.C.A.) was founded and their first race was held on 30 May at Freudenau. The races are open to professional and amateur jockeys, but owner-trainers have to consult professional trainers who are finally responsible for preparing the horses. One international race, preceded true to Austrian vivacity by a social event the pre vious evening, was held in September and it was won by Agar's Mach from the Netherlands.

As all breeders are aware, breeding a show champion to a show champion does not necessarily produce a top show winner. Many of the Austrian owners and breeders believe that it is vitally important to give full consideration to performance abilities, having found that those of typical halter pedigree can occasionally lack the iron stamina so necessary for performance. They feel that the basic Polish principle earlier referred to should be borne in mind: 'Without races there is no rational selection and without selection the degeneration and decline of each race of noble horses is inevitable.'

The philosophy of the A.R.C.A. foundation members is that Arabians are beautiful, but also tough and fast; they believe that breeding stallions should prove their ability in jumping or dressage, or in endurance or racing.

Ibn Naseeh (Naseeh Ibn Nazeerah ex Rubina), second in his class at the A.R.C.A. Futurity Show in Austria, had two wins and five places racing in 1994.

With this in mind the A.R.C.A. held its first Futurity Show for young Austrian Arabians at the race-track, designed to be an informal as well as a promotional event, in 1994. The Championship took place in between two races. To thus combine showing with racing is undoubtedly advantageous for the breed.

Nineteen horses were registered for racing and eleven races were held at Freudenau in 1994. A new attraction was the 'Futurity Cup', three races over short distances (1,400 to 1,800 metres) reserved for three and four year olds. International races were also organised.

Switzerland

The newly founded Swiss Arab Racing Club (S.A.H.R.C.) held its first official race for Arabians at the Basle Thoroughbred meeting on 13 July 1993. Twelve horses competed and, despite heavy rain, there was a good crowd and the betting turnover for the Arabian race was reported to be the highest of the day.

Seven more races for Arabians were held on Thoroughbred cards during the year, over distances ranging from 1,800 to 1,650 metres. The horses are professionally trained, in the same stables as Thoroughbreds. Two international races were held and both were won by French horses, but the Swiss-bred stallion Ibn Mareeba (Santorin ex Mareeba) was second at Frauenfeld. This race was the final one in which horses finishing fifth or better could accumulate points to contest the Veruska Trophy for the best Swiss Arabian Racehorse of the Year, which was awarded to Ibn Mareeba.

In 1994 the number of races was increased to 11, and 28 horses were registered in training. The Veruska Trophy was won by the mare Malisha who, interestingly, is closely related to Ibn Mareeba, being by Santorin out of Mashafa, a daughter of Mareeba.

Malisha had begun the season by winning a unique event – the first world-wide flat race of Arabians to be run on snow. The Veruska Arabians Snow World Challenge was run at St Moritz over a distance of 1,600 metres. It was open to W.A.H.O. recognised pure-breds, five year olds and over, since the organisers deemed it wise to allow only fully grown and experienced racehorses to compete in the gruelling race. Seven horses took part and Malisha won by six lengths with Ibn Mareeba in second place.

Belgium

As with most countries considering innovative sporting activities Arabian racing in Belgium was initiated by a small group of enthusiastic owners and

The Swiss mare Malisha who won the international race on snow at St Moritz in 1994.

breeders. After a few tentative efforts the Arabian Horse Racing Club of Belgium was founded in 1989 and the first races took place that year in Sterrebeek.

By 1992 there were only eight horses in training but the promoters felt that an initial period of teething problems was over when they received the support of the Belgian Jockey Club and encouragement from different Belgian racing societies. The leading horse that year was Hasan Bukari by Plakat out of Rafica and bred in Belgium.

It was decided to seek co-operation with the Netherlands and from 1993 Belgium has organised its racing in conjunction with the Dutch association, the D.A.R.C. The races are open to both countries and entrants can be trained by either an amateur or professional trainer or by the owner; jockeys can also be amateur or professional. Four race-tracks are used, three in the Brussels area and one in Ostend, and the races are included in official Thoroughbred meetings.

In 1994, eight races were held attracting from 7 to 18 runners. Although there were still only ten Arabians registered in training the number is expected to increase and at least 12 races took place in 1995.

Denmark

Enthusiasts of Arab racing in Denmark experienced difficulties when attempts were made to launch this new sport. The main problem was gathering together enough horses to make racing worth while. They maintain that a breakthrough came in 1987 when there were almost 20 horses in training and an international and also a Scandinavian race was held at Klampenborg, the oldest race-track in Scandinavia, and incidentally considered by many one of the most beautiful.

However, after that year the sport declined but happily interest revived in 1990 when seven races were held and 15 Arabians were in training. Matters progressed after this and in 1992 there were 44 horses in training and 20 races were run, three of them international. All the horses running that year were bred in Denmark, and many were sired by stallions which have produced show champions.

The Danish Jockey Club is keenly interested in helping to develop Arabian racing and co-operation with the Danish Arabian horse owners is said to work perfectly. Although the majority of trainers still hold amateur licences, training is professionally conducted and the horses are ridden by professional jockeys.

In 1994, 15 trainers were listed as having a total of 45 horses in training, 17 of which came from other countries. The leading horse was Silver Shah (Youri of Pelere ex Daisy), a nine-year-old stallion.

The Netherlands

During the 1980s a small number of enthusiasts started racing their Arabians but since 1990 the organisation has been on a professional basis under the Dutch Arabian Racing Committee (D.A.R.C.) in co-operation with the official authorities on Thoroughbred and Trotting Racing. Demonstration races on professional tracks initiated the rise in popularity of the sport and by 1993 up to 30 races were planned. The average turnover on betting is said to equal that of Thoroughbred racing.

Horses can be ridden by either professional or amateur jockeys and every owner/trainer has to consult a professional trainer on a regular basis during the racing season. In 1992 there were 72 Arabians in training and, although the races are open to foreign entrants, half the winners that year were bred in the Netherlands; horses of Russian blood-lines have had considerable influence.

Racing takes place at Duindigt, an 'A' racecourse near The Hague, usually at meetings for Thoroughbreds or trotters. In 1994, 101 Arabians were in training, 10 trainers were listed and 32 races held. The most successful mare was Zayna ES (Ghalil Abbelan ex Furno Femina) who in 15 starts had 9 wins and 3 places, giving her the title 'D.A.R.C. Horse of the Year 1994'. The leading stallion was Amir Moshari (Sherif Pasha ex Morasha) who in ten starts won three important international races and was placed five times.

Italy

Arab racing in Italy began in a small way in 1991, the races being limited to five horses only in each race. Encouraged by the success of these first efforts a much more ambitious programme was planned for 1992, with 40 races organised and run on five assorted courses. A highlight of the season was four races held during the Arabian Horse International B-Show at Grosseto, one of them being for part-breds. There were 68 horses in training in 1992.

France

France is distinct in having one of the most lengthy Arab racing histories, with official races first being held in 1860. In fact the French began breeding Arab racehorses during the last century, with three imported mares, Warda, Zulma and Arca, founding the main female lines. However, it was not until the beginning of the twentieth century that breeding establishments began to specialise in Arabian racehorses.

Since 1988 the Racing Committee of the French Arabian Horse Association has worked to develop more races for pure-breds only. Arab racing is organised on a professional basis in co-operation with the French Jockey Club. The results of these efforts is shown by the number of races increasing to 28 in 1992 with 81 horses in training. International meetings are popular; three were held at Evry, Fleurs and Craon, and the French Arabians, having been bred for their performance ability on the racecourse, are presently amongst the leaders in international racing in Europe, the U.S.A. and more recently in the Gulf States. This has obviously led to an increase in their value as racehorses and many of the leading French Arabians have been sold for high figures, mostly to Arab owners. Several of these have already been mentioned in the U.K. section. Stallions whose produce are especially in demand include Saint-Laurent, Gosse de Bearn, Manganate, Cheri Bibi and Dormane.

The Middle East

Flat racing and marathons

In the Middle East camel racing has long been a popular sport and is likely to continue so, but recently Marathon racing and horse versus camel races have become a feature. One school of thought asserts that competing over the longer distance (26¼ miles) of a Marathon is a better trial for the Arabian because it tests its stamina and courage as well as speed more realistically than does the comparatively short distance of flat racing. There is merit in this belief provided the race is run under proper veterinary supervision.

Nowhere has the recent revival of flat racing been as dramatic as in the Gulf and the United Arab Emirates. From 1990 the number of race meetings held and horses in training rose more rapidly than in any other part of the world. Huge crowds come to enjoy what is now a major sport, and with the ruling families investing enormous sums of money it has become in American terminology 'the racing industry'.

At the same time, with Arab sheikhs becoming principal purchasers of Arabian racehorses around the world and rivalling each other in competition on the track, prices paid for the fastest horses have escalated. This trend repeats the situation existing several years ago in the Arabian industry in the U.S.A. when enormous prices were paid for show champions – prices

The paddock at Dubai races.

far beyond the value in real terms of the horse itself and which have now dropped. The artificial nature of situations of this kind inevitably leads to increased production and then a surfeit, neither of which set of circumstances can be advantageous to the breed, or to the horses themselves, in the long term.

The first official horse race in the Emirates was held at Abu Dhabi on 11 November 1978, on the occasion of the Islamic Eid Al Adha holiday. This was followed by other races held to celebrate various important occasions such as the National Day, or to honour the visits of heads of state. An important event which took place on 16 April 1980 was the first Presidential Race.

In the early 1980s races were held also in Kuwait, Muscat and Bahrain. Many were to celebrate weddings of members of the ruling families of Abu Dhabi and Al Ain. Racing on the track at Umm Al Quwain began in April 1983, and for the next four years a few races were held each season in Abu Dhabi and Umm Al Quwain. Sharjah Equestrian Club had its first race in February 1987, and Ajman had a horse race on the camel track in January 1990. A few races continued to be held each season up to 1991.

In Qatar there has been Arabian racing for many years but here also it has escalated recently and now weekly race meetings are held during the season. Many of the horses taking part are imports from Russia, Egypt, Poland and the U.S.A. as well as some from the U.K. At every meeting there are races for Thoroughbreds and 'local bred' horses (of mixed origin but mainly Thoroughbred) as well as pure-bred Arabians.

Each country has a unique atmosphere to its racing; Oman, for instance, has trotters and exhibition camel sprints. In 1993 over 100 horses took part in several days of competitions at the oasis town of Bediya, bordering on the Wahiba sands, organised by the Oman Equestrian Federation. Entire families came to assist during the event and with pavilions for the reception and entertainment of visitors the result was a friendly and festive occasion. Included in the programme were long distance and pleasure rides and racing at the Al Safinat race-track.

Qatar has initiated its Desert Marathon run at the annual Festival of the Horse. Held for the first time in 1992 the Festival has become one of the most important events for Arabians in the Middle East, with a huge international attendance – the horses also are 'international' since a large proportion of them come from assorted overseas countries. The first two days are devoted to the show-ring, with championships held on the morning of the third day, the show now being held under E.C.A.H.O. rules. This is followed by racing on a grass track adjoining the showground.

As a grand finale the Desert Marathon run over 26 miles is held on the last day. In 1994 there were 38 starters. A halfway halt is obligatory where the horses are checked by vets and only allowed to continue when their heartbeat is down to 72. The winner of the race was the British-bred Anglo-Arab Granby Ironstone, by the Arabian Jabula out of Lady Dresden, with two pure-breds bred in Australia, who are acquitting themselves well in their new environment, Roynaz (Royalan ex Nazek) and Palexis (Milex ex Promissa), in second and third place.

Dubai also has its Marathon race. Brough Scott, writing in the *Sunday Telegraph*, described it as being strictly a local event, with only support vehicles and a few visitors, and 'a gymkhana, participant-centred feel. But a

ABOVE *Nu Toi (Numaa ex Toiloj), owned by Umm Qarn Farms, winner of the 1995 Qatar Marathon.*

ABOVE RIGHT *Granby Ironstone, owned by Sheikh Abdullah bin Khalifa Al Thani, winner of the 1994 Qatar Marathon and second in the U.K. Marathon in 1995. From 1991 to 1994 he raced in the U.K. over distances of six furlongs to two miles, winning eight times. In 1994 his record was three wins, second in the Sprint Championship and six thirds, out of ten starts.*

LEFT *Sheikh Rashid bin Hamdan Al Nahayan riding Roynaz at Al Asayl 40 km event in 1994.*

gymkhana from another world . . . of a strange mix of mediaeval customs, petro-dollar billions and new millennium technology which is at the heart of life in the Gulf.'

Starting by the border with Abu Dhabi, 40 horses raced over the 37 km of desert, with one compulsory walking section for a veterinary check, pursued by 'a hundred Range Rovers in the hunting pack bumping and grinding along the sand and scrub of the desert floor'. The finishing 'straight' is through a railed section quarter of a mile wide and 16 km in distance which was built in 1994 to accommodate horse-versus-camel racing – another sport enjoyed by the sheikhs, in which the victor is nearly always the horse.

One of the Abu Dhabi Royal Stables' Australian-bred Arabians was the winner by 16 seconds; his pace, checked by a vehicle's speedometer, disclosed he was doing 25 m.p.h. as he passed the finishing post to the triumphant honking of car horns, whilst the clock showed he had taken 60 minutes and 40 seconds to complete the course.

The reporter described how, after another five or six horses had finished, a great cry went up as a grey came careering through the dust, 'his tiny rider a bit wobbly in the saddle . . . As he passes the post a huge swirl of white smocks descend upon him and Sheykh Mohammed lifts him out of the saddle and gives him the kiss and the bear hug which tells of a delighted dad anywhere' – the miniscule jockey being his ten-year-old son. A far cry from the sedate paddocks of Ascot, Longchamp and Leopardstown, in three countries where Sheikh Mohammed had been leading Thoroughbred owner in 1994.

Dubai held its first flat-race meeting at the Metropolitan Equestrian Sports Centre in November 1991, but it was in 1992 that things really took off. The magnificent Jebel Ali race-track held its first meeting on 5 January, and the following month racing began at Nad Al Sheba race-track, which is now internationally famous.

In Abu Dhabi horse racing was organised by the Royal Stables up to 1992 and then by the Abu Dhabi Equestrian Club under the chairmanship of Sheikh Hazza Bin Zayed Al Nahayan. In 1993 the Equestrian Federation was set up with Sheikh Sultan Bin Khalifah Al Nahayan as chairman to control all equine sports activities in the U.A.E., but by 1994 racing had come under the Dubai Racing Association. This constant switch of authority reflects the swiftly changing scene in the Middle East, with even the names of race-tracks changing from year to year! There are now five race-tracks in the U.A.E. and with new trainers arriving on the scene every year racing is escalating at such a speed that it is almost impossible to keep up.

The first Arabians for racing and breeding were imported from Lebanon,

ABOVE *Sheikh Rashid bin Hamdan Al Nahayan's Alin (Djou Said ex Selena) winning at Nad Al Sheba, Dubai, in 1994.*

Bakarat, by Partner out of Bajeczka, owned by Sheikh Rashid bin Hamdan Al Nahayan, at Nad Al Sheba. From 34 starts he has won or been placed 21 times; he was also third in the stallion class at the 1995 Qatar International Show.

Jordan and Saudi Arabia in 1978, and these were followed by others from Iraq and Bahrain. A number of horses came from Morocco also, amongst them the stallion Magrabi, which is in fact of French breeding and has made a significant contribution to the breeding of successful racehorses in Abu Dhabi. These were followed by an influx of horses from the U.K., Germany, Russia and Holland, and more recently from France and the U.S.A. All the Arabians which race have to have a certificate of health and be registered in the W.A.H.O. Stud Book. In addition a large number of Thoroughbreds have been brought into the U.A.E. for racing.

The first jockeys to ride came from Pakistan in 1978 and four years later from Morocco. Now the jockeys riding are from most of the horse-racing countries around the world and several famous names in Thoroughbred racing have ridden Arabians in the Emirates. Many trainers also are from countries outside the Middle East, including several top young men from the U.S.A. and some from Britain.

Amongst some of the most successful horses are Dunaj (Aswan ex Monika) and Parafin (Naftalin ex Popitka). Locally bred horses have also had their successes, including Wasnan and Abiyan, both W.A.H.O. approved. In the 1993/94 season one of the best Arabians and winner of the big races was Unchainedd Melody (ZT Ali Baba ex Blu Bint Haleema), which was imported from the U.S.A. Vadeer, bred in the U.K. but with

Sheikh Zayed bin Sultan Al Nahayan's Unchainedd Melody leading the field at Abu Dhabi.

Russian-bred parents (Mamluk and Viola), has raced well and beaten some of the top horses, but in general it is the American-bred animals which are most successful in sprints and the French in the longer races. The imported horses are nearly always given Arabic names for racing, and unless one has access to the various Federations and Associations it is impossible to sort them out as no details of their breeding are given. In the Registry they are of course correctly entered under their original names.

With Arabians imported into the Middle East from North and South America and from Europe and then raced there and in Europe in the same year, there is a constant interchange of horses between all these countries. Arabian racehorses owned by the sheikhs have indeed come to live the lives of Thoroughbred racehorses.

Lebanon

Racing began in Beirut in 1895, according to John Tyrrel writing in *Country Life*. The Civil War which started in 1982 obviously caused a temporary cessation of this popular sport. A representative of the press is reported as saying that there were four principal elements which had to survive the war to ensure the continuance of civilised life in Beirut: the American University, the harbour, the airport and the race-track.

The Hippodrome has been the venue since 1918 but it suffered much damage in the war. Work began on re-building the area in 1990 and soon after racing re-commenced. By 1993 there were 150 owners and 600 horses, and race meetings were held every Sunday throughout the year. Nearly all the horses were stabled at the track, and trainers were licensed by the Society for the Protection and Improvement of the Arabian Horse in Lebanon. A board of 40 members controlled all aspects of racing, including technical services such as starting stalls, photo-finish and patrol cameras. Betting is supposed to be only on-track, using a French style pari-mutual, with the profit going to support the course and racing in general. However, illegal off-course betting has become something of a problem for it was reported that the local mafia were in control and taking 10 per cent of punter's winnings.

Most of the horses are bred at stud farms situated in the Akkar district, near Tripoli; two are owned by the Committee and the remainder are private. There are two classes of Arabian horse racing in Beirut: Class A for the 'absolutely pure breed' and Class B for 'those of lesser blood strains'. Horses which have run prominently on several occasions are inspected by the stewards who decide if they conform to the standards set for the Arabian breed.

U.S.A. and Canada

As in the case of nearly every country where the sport is not run by the State, the initiative to start Arabian racing in the U.S.A. came from a small group of enthusiastic breeders. According to Sandra Hibner, writing in *The Arabian Horse World*, the first race on a pari-mutual track was held on Armistice Day in 1959 when ten Arabians took part in an exhibition race at Laurel, Maryland. Further exhibition races were held at Pimlico, Maryland, on Thanksgiving Day, 1959, and at Tropical Park, Miami, in 1960. However, the betting interest is said to have waned due to the races being too long at two and a half miles and exhibition racing in the east died out.

In some western states, chiefly Arizona, Michigan and California, informal races began to be run during the 1960s at County Fairgrounds and at shows, with an occasional race on Thoroughbred tracks, but not during the Thoroughbred racing season. In 1966 two races were held at the U.S. National Arabian Horse Show, with the stipulation that in order to run in either the six furlong or one mile race horses had to be entered in a performance class at the show.

Racing in Oregon on a country fairground.

Sandra Hibner states that 'largely due to the efforts of the newly formed Arabian Horse Racing Association Arabians first raced pari-mutually at Evangeline Downs in Louisiana on September 2nd 1967'.

In her book *The Arabian War Horse to Show Horse*, Gladys Brown Edwards writes that races held under the auspices of the Arabian Horse Racing Association of America were the only ones where pari-mutual betting was allowed. The races were held on the same card as Thoroughbreds and the distances are given as six and a half furlongs to two miles. She says that for many years very few mares or fillies were raced but by the late 1970s a few races were being held for them and the 1979 I.A.H.A. Derby was won by a filly, El Camino Samira, by Joramir, who was named Race Filly of the Year. Her grandsire, Meteor (by Serafix) had raced and on her dam's side the horses were certainly multi-purpose, having been used for racing, endurance riding and in shows, as well as for work on the ranch. In those days the horses were raced at an older age and it was not unusual for Arabians to return to the race-track after a period of semi-retirement. One such was Al-Marah Ibn Indraff, who between 1959 and 1961 was placed behind Ofir (one of the top racehorses at that time) and returned to the race-track nine years later, again to be well placed in Phoenix. It is added that he won newspaper acclaim by being older than his jockey!

In the late 1960s two stallions dominated the racing scene: the Polish import Orzel and the American-bred Kontiki (Camelot ex Almiki). Kontiki was unbeaten until raced against Orzel, who later became National Champion side-saddle horse and Top Ten in halter. Kontiki, laid off for a period, was put back into training in 1971 and proceeded to win and break time records in races from six and a half furlongs to one and a half miles. He won every time out that year, culminating in the National Championship over two miles, carrying 149 lb. He also went on to the show-ring and the following year took a Reserve Championship at Scottsdale; Kontiki has proved a highly successful sire of racehorses.

There have been several official associations or committees organising Arabian racing in the U.S.A. and Canada. The former Arab Horse Racing Association of America was succeeded by the International Arabian Horse Association Racing Committee, whose chairman in 1975 was Dr Sam Harrison. He was an original member of the I.A.R.B. (International Arabian Racing Board), was a founder of the original Arabian Jockey Club in 1983 and presided over the Arabian Racing Cup Inc., a non-profit-making Tennessee Corporation. Its purpose was to promote Arab racing and one of its contributions was founding the Darley Awards in 1987 to honour top horses each year; it also founded the Arabian Cup, an event similar to the Thoroughbred Breeders Cup.

By 1979 the number of horses in training had reached 137 and prize money for the 70 races had amounted to $64,000. The great increase in the popularity of the sport, however, began in 1983 when the number of Arabians racing rose to over 200 and then rapidly increased each year until there were 835 in 1988. The number of races rose at the same time from 173 in 1983 to 536 in 1988, with prize money (purses) jumping up in the same period from $306,473 to $1,540,882. Racing now took place on official race-tracks on Thoroughbred or Quarter Horse cards, and on grass or dirt tracks. The body which now organises Arabian racing in the U.S.A. and Canada is the Arabian Jockey Club, which was officially chartered in 1987. It has the support of and works closely with the Arabian Horse Registry of America, and is a non-profit-making organisation dedicated to the professional management of the Arabian racing industry. It is responsible for promoting racing in North America as well as internationally; maintaining the official database of Arabian racing; encouraging a strong code of ethics and providing educational materials and seminars, as well as assisting the many state racing associations. It is these state associations which run the individual races.

Breed purity was one of the first concerns of the Jockey Club and they made it a top priority. In 1989 they began requiring parentage verification through blood testing, two years before it was put into use by the Arabian Horse Registry. Strict rules have been formulated for all Arabians before they can race. In addition to its Identification Supplement, issued by the Registry after the bloodtyping, each horse has to be tattooed on the inside of the upper lip with specific dyes by an agent of the Thoroughbred Racing Protective Bureau. This tattoo is verified before each race. After the race the winning horses, together with others chosen at random, go to the receiving barn for samples to be taken for urine and blood tests. If prohibited or unacceptable levels of drugs are found, the horse will be disqualified from that race.

Owners, as well as trainers, have to take out a licence and jockeys are all professionals. Arabians have to be three years old before they are allowed to race and this means that they will begin to be trained for racing in the autumn of their two-year-old year; starting with walking and trotting they are worked up to a slow gallop over a period of a month to two months.

Race distances are short compared to those in the U.K. Though varying from four and a half furlongs to one and three-quarter miles, the average is only six furlongs, but the A.J.C. is trying to discourage anything less than that distance. There are two main types of races, 'overnight', in which entries close less than three days before the start of the programme, and 'stakes', where the purse consists of nomination, entrance and starting fees, plus money added by the track itself. The top stakes races are graded according to the purse, number of runners and time of the race – some of the Arabian races are put on before the Thoroughbred section begins and as a result are less profitable because the smaller number of spectators means less betting revenue.

In line with its huge Arabian horse population, racing in North America has far outstripped the rest of the world in its scope, management and the number of horses in training – although, surprisingly, there are only just over twice as many racing Arabians registered as are in the U.K.; but four times as many races are held in the U.S.A. Arabian racing has certainly become 'an industry'. A number of auction sales take place each year. At the first Equest International sale held at Delaware Park in July 1993, top price of $210,000 was given for the unraced three year old Picasso WF (Piechur ex Gilza) to go to Umm Qarn, Qatar. With horses in training, brood mares and two year olds on offer the overall average price was $25,300 and the bottom price $1,050.

The year 1993 proved to be a record-breaking one with the number of Arabians participating topping the 1,000 mark for the first time. Statistics showed that Arabian racing appeared to be maturing into an industry comparable to other major racing breeds. For 1994 races were planned in 15 states, with California leading the way, as well as in Alberta, Canada. Since Canadian racing comes under the A.J.C. the statistics include that country; in fact only 17 races were held in Canada and 706 in the U.S.A.

Even though the average owner won more prize money in 1994 and the betting handle also increased, there was a slight decrease in the number of races run, and Arabians taking part fell to 948. According to a study conducted by the Arabian Horse Registry this reflects the general downturn in the population of registered horses born in 1990 and 1991. However, despite this overall decline in breeding the number of 1993 foals by leading racehorse sires rose dramatically, whilst the total number of foals born fell by 4.8 per cent. The A.J.C. is looking to growth in the sport in 1996.

The leading sire for 1994 was Wiking, helped by the success of WF Wincent, winner of the Drinkers of the Wind Futurity. In second place was Samtyr (Sambor ex Tryncza) who is still top of the list of all-time leading sires. A brilliant horse himself, Samtyr was the 1975 Champion Racehorse.

It is impossible here to give all the names of the numerous Arabians who have achieved greatness in American racing. However, mention should be made of two outstanding full sisters by ZT Ali Baba out of Blu Bint Haleema. Victorias Secrett, Horse of the Year in the Darley Awards for 1992, was still unbeaten after 12 races when she took on the colts in the 1993 Armand Hammer and won by four lengths. She was purchased by Sheikh Mohammed Bin Rashid Al Maktoum early in 1992 for what was then considered the staggering price of $425,000. The equally brilliant younger sister, Unchainedd Melody, dominated the scene as a three year old as strongly as her sister had the previous season; she was then sold to Sheikh Mansoor bin Zayed al Nahayan for a reported two million dollars and has become one of the top racehorses in the U.A.E.

Other countries

Arabian racing now takes place in many countries around the world. Whilst it is well established in Europe, the U.S.A. and in the Middle East, it is also becoming an important sport in many other areas.

Argentina

Arabian racing was launched by the Arabian Breeders' Arab Horse Association in 1989, when the first race was held on 1 November at the San Isidro Hippodrome. With the support of the Jockey Club Racing Commission, and backed by some of the best professional trainers and jockeys, this new venture was heralded with enthusiasm and became an instant success.

The winner of the race, over 2,000 metres, was Moro Famoso (Sayang ex Fuga) in what was then claimed as a record time of 2 minutes 14.1 seconds. Moro Famoso was a brilliant racehorse and became Arab Racehorse of the Year for three successive years from 1989 to 1991, before being sold and exported to Abu Dhabi. LC Daruk (Duke of Nafir ex Na-Run), from the same stable, won the title in 1992.

Although the number of Arabians in training for racing was not large – less than 100 – their excellent performances became internationally recognised. Biphar went to the U.S.A. where he ran successfully and was then bought for the President of the United Arab Emirates. Many others have been exported and continued their successes in other countries.

Racing in Argentina is now flourishing. Nineteen races were held in 1994 on three different courses near Buenos Aires on days when Thoroughbreds were racing. The size of the fields ranged from seven to nineteen, with the number of runners in most races going into double figures.

Australia

The Western District Arabian Riders and Breeders began holding an Annual Race Meeting in 1985 on a track at Burrumbeet. Started as a purely amateur sport as an outlet for many of the geldings (in Australia far more colts are gelded than is the case in European countries), it was also intended to give good promotion for the breed. Some of the Arabians taking part combined racing with endurance.

In 1988 the Central Victorian Arabian Racing and Action Club held its inaugural meeting. A second meeting the following year was held at Rochester Racecourse when eight races were run, one of them being a (ridden) trotting race for juniors. Three of the races were for part-breds and, of the remaining four for pure-breds, one was a junior sprint over 300 metres, two were sprints of 600 metres, and the principal race for the Pure-bred Cup was over 1,500 metres.

Horses often ran in two races at the same meeting, as sometimes happened in the U.K. in the early days. At Rochester the pure-bred stallion Kevisan Park Zivago (Sindhel ex Najani) won both the Cup and the Sprint.

At the fifth Annual Western District Race meeting at Barrumbeet in 1989, 18 horses participated and two won twice. Excellent racing was reported with the Challenge Cup, run over 1,400 metres, being won for the second successive year by the eight-year-old part-bred gelding Lancefield Springtime (El Ramadin ex Ashfield Lady). For these wins he carried off the Carrington Cup, a perpetual trophy for the best performer in Victorian Arab Racing. A week later Lancefield Springtime took part in a 160 km endurance ride!

A great leap forward was made in 1994 when seven pure-bred Arabians ran for the first time at Flemington Racecourse as part of the Second National Horse Expo. The object was to give a demonstration gallop to promote the Arabian horse, as well as to encourage racing. The winner was the ten-year-old gelding Avondale Pirouette (Akhu ex Arkab Dancer). After the race the four stallions and three geldings taking part were presented with sashes by the Minister for Racing. To coincide with this the Victorian Arabian Jockey Club was formed. This group now organises Arabian racing within Victoria. Up to the end of 1994 the races run in conjunction with Thoroughbred race meetings were categorised as just demonstration gallops.

On 2 September seven Arabians took part in another exhibition race over 1,000 metres at the Seymour Cup Day meeting; it was won by Fenwick Cazique with Eleaffar Cadenza second. The following month North East Arabians, an action club in Victoria, staged an Arabian Exhibition Race at the Benalla Cup Day meeting on 10 October. Fenwick Cazique was again the winner; second was Omani Shazah, with Eleaffar Cadenza in third place. Fenwick Cazique, a nine-year-old gelding by El Serene out of Crepe de Chine, is a well-known contestant in the show-ring, having won championships in-hand and reserve championships under saddle. This versatile character also competes in dressage, eventing, show-jumping, costume, stockhorse and western pleasure, and in his spare time enjoys rounding up cattle and sheep at home!

As part of the exhibition on each occasion the runners were led on to the track by riders mounted on Arabians in full Arab costumes. As a result of the interest generated by these races Thoroughbred racing clubs have been inviting Arabian horse owners to run at their meetings.

Leanne Quinlan and Fenwick Cazique after winning the Arabian Demonstration race at Benalla, Australia, 1994.

So far there have been no rules regarding the status of jockeys or trainers. Some horses are trained and ridden by professional trainers/riders, while others are trained and ridden by their owners.

More races were held in 1995, including one on the famous Flemington track, and racing clubs came into being in New South Wales and Queensland. With interest in the sport growing rapidly throughout the country, the National Arabian Racecourse Association was formed in 1995, to work with the state clubs over the organisation and promotion of racing.

South Africa

There has been a limited amount of racing in South Africa for some years. It is reported to have declined in the Transvaal in recent years, but in the

Western Cape amateur meetings are held bi-monthly at Durbanville, where there is an excellent racecourse with full facilities run by the Amateur Cape Hunt and Polo Club.

In 1994 a movement began to encourage participation by Arabian horse owners. The horses were ridden by riders in traditional costume and a close finish between three runners was recorded in one race. Races at professional race meetings have now been promised, provided that at least ten fit and well-trained horses are present. Enthusiastic owners who believe that racing provides the ultimate performance test for the Arabian are sponsoring these new efforts to get the sport going in South Africa.

Morocco

In 1988 six races were held for Arabians in Morocco. This has now escalated and in 1994 there were 68 official races organised by the Royal Jockey Club on courses at Rabat, Casablanca, Setta and El Jadida and over 150 pure-breds bred in Morocco took part. A new national training centre to be opened with facilities to train over 200 horses will include many pure-breds.

CHAPTER FIVE

Endurance riding

THERE CAN BE LITTLE doubt that the Arabian is the breed *par excellence* for endurance riding. Its unique physical attributes (explained in Chapter 2), combined with characteristic generosity and willingness to give the utmost to its human partner have made it by far the most popular choice for endurance riders. There are, of course, horses of other breeds which have excelled in endurance but most of these can be found to carry Arabian blood in their veins. Experts can often spot a certain *type* of horse which is likely to prove best for endurance. Their findings are certainly borne out, for the Arabian, being an extremely prepotent breed when crossed with others, has the ability to transmit through many generations common denominators essential for this work.

Feats of endurance by Arabians have a long history. Many of the verses and tales of the Bedouin tribesmen, recited as part of oral traditions for hundreds of years down the generations, extol the heroic deeds of horse and rider. Countless instances are cited of the courage, speed and endurance of the horses both in warfare and life itself in the harsh environment of the desert. Modern endurance riding records only serve to endorse the position of the Arabian and its derivatives as the favourite mount for this fast-growing sport, which is now enjoyed in no fewer than 53 countries.

Around the turn of the century rides were organised on the Continent as a project to test cavalry mounts, but generally there was no supervision of the condition of the horses and many died as a result of insufficient fitness when undergoing the rigours of being ridden strenuously over long distances.

In Britain in 1920 the newly formed Arab Horse Society held a 300 mile Endurance Test and this and similar events held in the U.S.A. at about the same time could be viewed as forerunners of modern endurance races. The Arab Horse Society Test was held at Lewes in Sussex and was ridden over five consecutive days, with careful veterinary supervision. It was won by Shahzada (Mootrub ex Ruth Kesia), a stallion destined to become famous for his prowess in this sphere and later, after exportation to Australia, as a show champion and sire. A similar event held in 1921 was won by the mare Belka (Rijm ex Bereyda), with Shahzada in second place. In the third Test organised by the A.H.S. the following year Shahzada won again. Thereafter no more endurance races were held by the A.H.S. until 1965.

The grey Shahzada and Robin, first and second in the 1920 Arab Horse Society Endurance Test.

ELDRIC and the F.E.I.

H. V. Musgrave Clark on Belka in the Arab Horse Society Endurance Test, 1921.

The popularity of endurance riding as an equestrian discipline on the continent of Europe started in the 1970s, and several countries formed associations to foster the sport. It became apparent, however, that many of the rules drawn up by different countries were at variance. The danger of horses being overridden through ignorance, together with insufficient veterinary attendance in some instances, was a cause for concern. So it was that in 1979 riders from seven European nations (France, Great Britain, Germany, Italy, Portugal, Spain and Switzerland) came together to found the European Long Distance Rides Conference (ELDRIC). This was to prove a milestone in the development of endurance riding, not only in Europe but throughout the world.

ELDRIC's main concern was the protection of horses against being ridden too hard by ambitious riders and to this end rules were formulated. Prime intentions were to educate riders, vets and organisers in the field of endurance and to promote veterinary research into the various aspects of the effects of long distance work on horses participating. In addition the rules contained minimal requirements for all rides counting towards a special award, the ELDRIC Trophy, which is judged on a points system and is now one of the most coveted awards in endurance riding. To be placed, a rider has to complete three rides on the same horse in at least two countries.

Inevitably there were some teething problems as ELDRIC wanted to establish consistent guidelines for both riders and horses throughout Europe; but these difficulties were successfully overcome and in 1982 the first set of statutes was unanimously accepted. ELDRIC grew steadily and in 1994 there were 20 full members and 8 associate members – including Argentina, Australia, Canada, New Zealand, South Africa and the U.S.A. The ELDRIC Trophy contained 54 rides in 17 different countries; of 1,208 starters about 50 per cent finished.

At the same time that ELDRIC was becoming established a working Committee of the F.E.I. (Fédération Equestre Internationale) was setting up the rules for endurance riding, having in 1981 officially accepted endurance riding as an international equestrian sport. Although ELDRIC wanted to co-operate it was not an F.E.I.-recognised body; also some disagreements existed, the main one being that the F.E.I. considered that a small amount of Butazolidine, the anti-inflammatory, was permissible for a competing horse whereas ELDRIC was against any medication. Nevertheless some endurance riders were invited to the last meeting of the working committee.

Later in 1983 Dr Georg Riedler, then President of ELDRIC, went to Rome for discussions with Professor Vittorio de Sanctis of the F.E.I. who was in charge of setting up their endurance rules. This proved to be a highly successful meeting with both men agreeing that they had the same ideals for endurance riding. A few weeks later the F.E.I. agreed to ban all medication at endurance rides and the first set of Rules for Endurance Riding was drawn up. From 1990 to 1995 Dr Riedler was Chairman of the F.E.I. Endurance Sub-Committee, which is composed mainly of endurance riders and veterinary surgeons from three continents, with ELDRIC represented by at least two members.

The co-operation between the F.E.I. and ELDRIC has greatly facilitated recognition of the growing importance of the sport of endurance riding. The F.E.I., as the international governing body for equestrian disciplines, establishes rules which are effective world-wide; its members are National Equestrian Federations. In 1984 the F.E.I. introduced the first European

Endurance Championship, in France; in 1986 the first North American Endurance Championship, in the U.S.A., and also the first World Championship, in Rome, Italy. In 1990 the World Equestrian Games, held in Sweden, included endurance for the first time.

ELDRIC's role is to organise conferences and seminars, publish news and a yearbook and encourage contacts on a general basis; its members are European Endurance Associations. In addition it runs the ELDRIC Trophy which, for the first time in 1994, was entirely to F.E.I. rules and is accepted by the F.E.I. as the F.E.I./ELDRIC Trophy.

Since the Trophy was first awarded in 1980 it has been won nine times by British riders, three times by Germans, twice by French and once by a Swiss and an Italian (there was a tie in 1983).

It is interesting to note that up to 1994 no ELDRIC trophy winner had won an F.E.I. or European World title, the inference being that it rewards consistency rather than the exceptional individual win.

Although there has been a tremendous advance in endurance riding during the last decade with increased winning speeds and fewer eliminations, there are some who feel that more emphasis needs to be put on the importance of completing and presenting a fit horse after the ride.

Great Britain

In 1965 the A.H.S. decided to instigate long distance riding once again and held a two-day Trial at Goodwood. Competitors rode 50 miles on the first day and then took part in a Prix Caprilli test on the second. Successful entrants were awarded First- or Second-Class Premiums and of the six horses to gain top honours, five were pure-bred Arabians. That same year the British Horse Society organised the first Golden Horseshoe Ride, over 50 miles on Exmoor.

The idea behind the A.H.S. Two-day Trial was to test not only the stamina of the horses but their suppleness after completing 50 or 75 miles of stiff cross-country riding carrying a minimum of 11 stone. For the second Trial held the following year, marks were given for time and dressage and also by the veterinary surgeon following a rigorous inspection. Once again the top-placed horses were pure-breds, with two well-known stallions, Marino Marini (Mikeno ex Roshara) and Kami (Iridos ex Kabara), being first and second.

In 1968 the A.H.S. was invited by the B.H.S. to join in the organisation of the Golden Horseshoe Ride and this was held in conjunction with special ridden classes for A.H.S. members. Part-breds came to the fore that year, when eight of the first ten placings in the Golden Horseshoe were of Arab breeding. For the next six years the two Societies continued to work together and the Golden Horseshoe Ride was lengthened from 50 to 75 miles; later a 100 mile class was added.

In 1975 the B.H.S., recognising the importance of the sport within its many activities, formed its Long Distance Riding Group (L.D.R.G). Now the L.D.R.G. organises a full series of rides, graduated so that riders and

Pause for refreshment: Silver Rabba and Kate McIver, 1994 Golden Horseshoe Ride.

horses can progress through short undemanding ones to the extremely challenging strenuous events. However, a Golden Horseshoe is still one of the most coveted awards and this type of ride, requiring performance to a set standard to obtain an award, rather than the concept of coming first, second or third, has continued to be highly popular with competitors.

Two years before the L.D.R.G. was formed two enterprising people, Ann Hyland and Alan Exley, had decided to form a group to organise rides for the growing number of enthusiastic long distance riders. Thus in 1973 the Endurance Horse and Pony Society of Great Britain (E.H.P.S.) came into being. It grew rapidly from running a wide selection of pleasure and competitive rides to holding the first 100 miler in England, the Summer Solstice, so-named because of the date, 21 June, of the first Ride in 1975.

The E.H.P.S. now organises a great number of events from Pleasure Rides of 15 to 20 miles, to Competitive Trail Rides, similar to those run in the U.S.A. and of distances ranging from 20 to 60 miles, with the ride category determined by the speed set and judging done on a time-plus-condition basis. The most demanding are the Endurance Rides for which horses have to upgrade from C.T.R.s and must be a minimum of six years old, or seven before they can enter a 100 miler, and qualify by completing certain L.D.R.G. or E.H.P.S. rides. These Endurance Rides vary from 40 to 100 miles.

Horses in the U.K.

Endurance is the discipline in which partnerships forged between horse and rider are of the greatest importance and for this reason the rider's name is given with that of the horse in the following sections.

Over the years many pure-bred, Anglo and part-bred Arabs have made their mark in long distance riding; there are far too many to mention more than a few of them here. Ann Hyland's stallion Nizzolan (Lewisfield Nizzamo ex Solange), imported from the U.S.A. when his owner returned to England in 1968, was an outstanding horse in the early days of competitive riding. He won the first Summer Solstice and the High Points Trophy for the leading endurance horse in 1974 and 1975, after which he appeared in the Parade of Champions at the Horse of the Year Show; he has also sired several good long distance horses.

The British team of four in the first World Championships at Rome in 1986 consisted of three pure-breds, Carole Tuggey's gelding El Askar (Tombolo ex Kismet III), Denise Passant's mare Ferhanoush (Farif ex Indian Velvet) and Val Long's stallion Tarim (Luachim ex Tari); the fourth member of the team was the three-quarter Thoroughbred mare, Forest Fox, owned by Pam Jones. Fourteen of the 50 riders finished the race, and in an exciting and very close finish between three horses for second position Tarim was eventually given fourth place. Ferhanoush was unfortunately spun lame before the finish but Forest Fox and El Askar came in sixth and ninth respectively and enabled Britain to win the team Gold Medal.

Tarim was the first to beat Nizzolan's winning time in the Summer Solstice when he won in a remarkable 9 hours 49 minutes in a speed of 10.1 m.p.h. around Sherwood Forest in 1984. He was selected three years in succession to represent his country and he also won the Summer Solstice three times, coming in top place in 1986 and 1988 as well. In 1986 Tarim was awarded the A.H.S. Sports Horse of the Year title in recognition of his outstanding record in long distance. He too is the sire of top-class endurance horses, including Rani Tarina, out of Romanina. The other two pure-breds in the team at Rome also had distinguished careers. El Askar had an exceptional record as he completed over 2,000 miles in competition in his first five full seasons without ever being eliminated from a ride – a wonderful achievement which pays tribute to his owner's careful training and riding. His numerous wins include the Goodwood International 100 miler three times, the 200 km Ride at Montcuq in France, plus a best condition award, three Golden Horseshoes and an outright win in the 1985 Distance Rider National Championships for points accrued in both E.H.P.S. and L.D.R. rides. In 1986 he won the ELDRIC Trophy with Tarim in second place.

Ferhanoush won a number of best condition awards and came third overall at Montcuq in 1986. Known as 'Deux Jours de Montcuq' this 120 mile ride in the south of France is held over two days. It is one of the sport's oldest and most prestigious rides and is described as being arduous not only because of the longer than usual distance and the testing hills around Cahors, but because of the speed at which it is run. After a very good season in 1988 Denise Passant won the ELDRIC Trophy with Ferhanoush.

Young riders

Arabians are frequently ridden by junior riders and one very successful combination in the early days of the sport was that of Jackie Ware and the stallion Cairo (Indriss ex Castanea). Jackie started riding him in junior events when she was 14 and won many high point trophies. The following year she upgraded to stiffer competition in open rides, winning the Red Dragon Ride in Wales and becoming the 1978 Reserve Arab Champion. Jackie had the distinction of being at that time the youngest rider to win an open endurance event in Britain and in 1979 she took the Open Championship, in addition to being Junior Champion.

In 1989 the British National Championship was won by another young rider, Claire Brown, then aged 19, with her pure-bred mare, Shireen Lailee (Paradazy ex Lady Shamrock). Nic Wigley won her first Junior Championship in 1990 at the age of 16 with her pure-bred gelding, Marbat (Haroun ex Mahbubat Bint Al Malik), and on their first international event won the Belgian Condroz Ride, thus helping Great Britain to take the Team Trophy for the fourth consecutive year. Saskie Lovell was also 16 when she was B.H.S. Junior Champion in 1994 with her part-bred Pensilva Sparkle. The following year they took the Championship again in a close finish at the Dukeries Ride, completing the 60 miles at a very fast average speed of 12.90 m.p.h.

Part-bred Arabs

For the World Championships held in the U.S.A. in 1988, 17 of the 22 horses on the initial list for the British team had Arab blood. The final selection was Tarim; Margaret Wilkes' Wyere Lad, a part-bred by Sollum who for two years running had won the 100 mile Red Dragon Ride, was fourth in the 1987 Marathon and won the 1988 Goodwood International 100 miles; Candy Cameron's part-bred White Trooper, by White Falcon, who was fifth in the same Marathon and also won a Golden Horseshoe and came second in the 1988 Summer Solstice; and Stephanie Nash's Gemini, another part-bred of Thoroughbred/Arab/Welsh breeding, who later won the 1989 Summer Solstice.

Wyere Lad and White Trooper finished in sixth and seventh positions, only 49 minutes behind the leader, American Becky Hart and RO Grand Sultan (Sultan El Shiko ex EZ Shariene), and Gemini came in sixteenth, but at the final vetting the following morning Britain's hopes for a Silver Medal were dashed when White Trooper was spun for lameness. However, 1991 was a good year for Candy Cameron and White Trooper. They took one of the only three Gold Awards at the Golden Horseshoe Ride,

Candy Cameron on White Trooper.

clocking the fastest time over the two day 100 mile course and receiving the prize for the horse most able to continue for a further 25 miles. They also won the Scottish Championship and finished the season winning the Red Dragon Ride of 130 miles over three days in the mountains of mid Wales. Still going strong in 1994, White Trooper won the Home International two day 100 mile class over the Yorkshire Dales to lead the Scottish Team to an overall win.

International riders and horses

Cathy Brown, who is based in France but frequently competes in and rides for Britain, has had much success with her pure-bred stallion, Naquib (Dahman ex Jamila). He finished first at Montcuq in 1986 and the next year led all the way to win the Goodwood International 100 Mile Ride over two days, and also won the Braemer 50 Mile Ride. This event has excellent going and has produced some of the fastest speeds in British endurance rides.

The 1989 Summer Solstice held at Ludlow drew a huge entry of 56 competitors. Behind the winner, Stephanie Nash and Gemini, there were several international horses in the top placings. Marcy Pavord, writer and endurance rider, wrote that 'the overwhelming percentage of Arabian blood in this "top ten" speaks volumes for the supremacy of the breed in the sport'.

That year Cathy introduced another stallion, King Minos (Impresario ex Yirene). It is said by the experts that it takes three years for an endurance horse to reach his prime and certainly 1992 became a great year for the ten-year-old King Minos. Second at the Barcelona dress rehearsal for the World Championships, when Cathy wisely did not push him in a tight finish, they won a brilliant victory at Lucerne in the 100 mile William Tell Race and ended the season winning the French Ride at Montcuq and Best Condition Award; not surprisingly, they won the ELDRIC trophy and Arab Horse Award. One of the reasons King Minos has had such great success is attributed to his exceptional cardiac recovery rate which enables him to get through vet gates rapidly.

Yvonne Tyson's pure-bred gelding Crystal Calif (Crystal Comet ex Flame of Destiny) was the B.H.S. L.D.R. National Champion in 1988 and the following year won the Belgian Condroz Ride. In 1992 he triumphed again on the Continent winning the ELDRIC 80 miler in Brittany and coming equal first in the 75 mile L'Ardennaise Ride in Belgium.

Second to Crystal Calif in the 1989 Condroz Ride was another pure-bred gelding who has also represented Britain internationally, Ibriz (El Khursan ex Clear Blue), belonging to Jane Donovan. Ibriz, quoted as being 'a superb

Cathy Brown and King Minos at Barcelona, 1992 World Championships.

ambassador for the performance aspects of the breed', won the individual Silver Medal at the 1990 World Equestrian Games at Stockholm and only just missed a medal in the 1991 European Championships at Montelimar. The notorious course for this event had been changed and included more flat going with the result that speed was the telling factor, but Jane and Ibriz finished only two minutes after the third horse, with a long gap behind them to the rest of the field. The A.H.S. High Point Award went to Ibriz that year, with King Minos a close second.

The final selection for the British team for the 1990 World Equestrian Games was made after minor mishaps caused Crystal Calif to be withdrawn just before the ride, and Ibriz to be relegated to individual status, due to being cast in his stable a month before the games and the resulting leg injury still needing to be bandaged to cover the healing wound, although he was completely sound and fully fit. In the event Great Britain was represented by three part-bred Arabs: General Portfolio Hero, of Thoroughbred/Arab/Irish Draught breeding, owned by Joy Loyla; Lilla Walls and Alfie, by the pure-bred Raffyk out of an Irish Cob mare; and Judith Heeley with Shumac, believed to be an Arab/Welsh cross.

Lilla Wall and Alfie on Beacon Hill in the Quantocks, South Wales in the background.

After a race full of tension the British team regained their status as World Champions and brought home the Gold Medal, the only one to be won by Britain throughout the games and, with Ibriz's individual Silver, the endurance horses and riders won well-deserved acclaim. General Portfolio Hero gave a superb performance to head the British team and Shumac finished in the top ten, but the hero of the day was Alfie. He surprised everyone by producing the speed to finish sixth and in doing so overhauled the French team, who then made such a determined effort to win the title that two of their horses were eliminated at vettings and one failed to complete the course. Alfie also won the ELDRIC Best Condition award. The previous year he had been third in the Belgian Condroz and took the ELDRIC Trophy; in 1991 he won the Fontwell International Ride. General Portfolio Hero was the 1989 E.H.P.S. Manar Trophy winner.

Jill Thomas's pure-bred Egyptian Khalifa (Egyptian Pharoah ex Sahara Khadine) was fourth in the 1988 Summer Solstice and it was predicted then that he would soon feature at international level. Two years later he won the Belgian Condroz Ride and was a member of the winning British Team;

Jill Thomas with Egyptian Khalifa at the World Championships, Barcelona, 1992.

he also won a Golden Horseshoe award and the coveted Wilkinson Sword Trophy awarded to the winner at the Summer Solstice. After such a successful season it was not surprising that he was awarded the A.H.S. Ferishal Trophy for the pure-bred Arabian gaining most points during 1990. More was to come, however, for at the 1993 European Championships held at Southwell Jill and Egyptian Khalifa won the Individual Gold and established a new British and European record of 11.5 m.p.h.

King Minos won the individual Bronze and Denise Passant with Soneri (Sun Prince ex Nagiba) led the winning British team and won the Best Condition Award. In 1994 Egyptian Khalifa was the highest placed British horse in the European Championship, finishing in ninth place, and confirming his position in the top ten of endurance horses.

The 1994 World Equestrian Games held at The Hague provided an entirely new type of going, over flat country in an urban area, with some of the course through deep sand dunes, and the final part along busy streets. It was considered a very severe course, a view borne out by the completion rate of only 54 per cent, compared with 63 per cent at Southwell in 1993.

The efforts of the French team, which had undertaken several training weekends and had worked at The Hague, paid off as they completely dominated the scene and took the Team Gold. The former French champion, Denis Pesce, won the individual Silver Medal riding his 16-year-old Selle Français Melfinik, who is by the Arabian, Persik. However, the individual Gold went once again to America who have an unbroken record, having won the title since the first official World Championships were held in 1986. Three times World Champion Becky Hart with her brilliant pure-bred RO Grand Sultan was sadly one of the victims of the difficult going, suffering a fall with damage to the horse's knees and subsequent elimination at the third vet gate. But compatriot Valerie Kanavy on her 12-year-old pure-bred Pieraz was a worthy successor, coming in six minutes ahead of Melfenik and also taking the best condition award.

Winner for the second successive year of the 1994 Summer Solstice was Jackie Taylor with her 12-year-old Anglo-Arab/Trakehner mare, Sally. The previous year they set a new British record of 10.46 m.p.h. and were almost as fast this year, riding through the Lincolnshire wolds and cantering in easily 51 minutes ahead of their nearest rivals; they also took the Best Condition award. A brilliant year for this pair who won at Montcuq and took both the British Open and British National titles (the first to achieve this double in the same year), their reward being the F.E.I./ELDRIC Trophy.

With many good young horses coming on, a strong contingent of junior riders, and with competition for the junior titles hotly contested, the future for Britain in endurance riding looks promising.

In 1994 a novice team all riding horses with Arabian blood competed in Belgium's toughest ride, the Ardennaise. The ride developed into a two-horse race, with 20-year-old Karen Vernon on Wheal Buller George finishing just in front of Jo Trego with Oliver's Taboo (Legionnair ex Shareema), who took the best condition award; they were 46 minutes ahead of the Belgian Françoise Minguet on Graveline.

At the 1995 European Endurance Championships held in Brittany, the British team beat the reigning World Champions on their home ground and retained their position as European Champions. The team of four included Oliver's Taboo, who finished fifth overall, and Egyptian Khalifa, sixth, representing his country for the fifth successive year. Earlier Oliver's Taboo had won his third Golden Horseshoe and the coveted Premier Award for the horse most capable of going a further 25 miles.

Archimedes, ridden by Lesley Caswell, with the grey Tarka (Marino Marini ex Tia Maria), High Point Arabian in the E.H.P.S. for 1994.

Endurance riding, due maybe to its long-drawn-out nature over varied terrain, is unlikely to be the spectator sport in the way that racing is, so sadly the horses and riders who compete so brilliantly in this discipline do not get the degree of publicity they deserve. The Arabians which compete in endurance are those that best exemplify many characteristics of the breed; perhaps breeders might bear this in mind when they consider their aim. Long distance rides are excellent tests and an Arabian of high quality which can win in the show-ring and then go on to become a successful endurance horse must be near to the ideal.

Europe

The Netherlands

One of the earliest official long distance riding tests to be held on the Continent of Europe involving an Arabian horse took place in the Netherlands on 6 July 1935. It was organised by members of the Stadskanaal Riding Club of the Netherlands, and the course was over 60 km of mostly turf with some roads. There were compulsory halting places, including one at the finish when all horses had to be examined by a panel of three vets. Competitors operated in teams of four, but the Committee invited T.H. Barlagen to enter his recently imported Arabian stallion Akal (Shelook ex Almas), bred in England by C.W. Hough, to compete as an individual.

Eleven teams were entered and the members of the Club chose four horses which in their considered opinion gave the best performances – two Hanoverians and two Groninger-Oldenburgers. There were no weight restrictions. None of the Club's team carried more than 14 stone; Akal, however, carried 17¾ stone.

Excluding time at the halts, Akal's travelling time was 3 hours and 16 minutes, whilst the first team home (the Studskanaal) took 3 hours and 35 minutes. The next five teams to complete took from two to two and three-quarter hours longer. Akal's temperature at the start was 101.5, he covered the first 20.5 miles in 1 hour 47 minutes, and on arrival at the first halt his temperature was 103.7. After ten minutes' rest he set off again and on arrival at the second halt his temperature was 102.1. Fifteen minutes later he started on the last stage and on his arrival at the finish his temperature was back to 101.5. The main point of interest lay in the vets' remarks on the horses' condition at the finish. Akal's condition was rated as 'absolutely perfect'; the Stadskanaal team were 'not quite satisfactory' and the next five teams were pronounced 'very bad', 'not quite satisfactory', 'worse', 'somewhat better' and 'worse'.

Whilst it was agreed that 37¼ miles was not a great test the conclusion drawn was that Akal's vastly superior performance, carrying a far greater weight, 'was a result that even an Arab horse could be proud of'.

This instance is given as it is historically interesting to find in detail a description of an endurance test in Europe of over 50 years ago.

It was not until 1984 that endurance riding began officially in the Netherlands with an annual ride over a distance of 90 km. Since 1991 four to five rides of 80 km or over are held, currently run by the N.V.L.R. One Dutch rider whose pure-bred Arabian Jashin has proved his versatility and also reached the top in endurance is Yvonne van de Velde.

Yvonne says that she grew up with Jashin as she bought him as a yearling with her very first salary when she was 17. Beginning with dressage, which she maintains is the best initial training for any performance horse, they later moved on to jumping, hunting, and even racing, before starting endurance. In 1991 they won the ELDRIC Arab Horse Trophy and were third in the Rider/Horse Combination, though still continuing to compete in international freestyle dressage to music.

Belgium

Official endurance riding in Belgium began earlier than in the Netherlands, the first four rides taking place in 1980. The regulations are similar to those of Britain and Germany, although the Belgian Highway Code bans riders of 13 and under on roads, so junior competitors must be over that age.

One of the best known Belgian riders is Dominique Crutzen, who started competing with his half-Arab gelding Comino de Sier in 1984. They were the only Belgian pair to complete the first World Championships, where they came eleventh. In 1986 they were fourth in the ELDRIC Trophy and after many more successes became the European Champions when winning at Montelimar in 1991.

Norway

Long distance riding in Norway has its roots in a sport in which cavalry officers participated over a century ago. A legacy left by a young Norwegian officer who died in 1885 also links the Middle East with modern endurance riding.

Thomas Stang-Michelet, a cavalry officer, had enlisted under the British flag to serve in the Sudan. Before joining his English regiment he travelled to Egypt and took part in a ride with Bedouins which lasted several days. He suffered sunstroke and typhus and was to die in hospital, but before his death he had willed 20,000 Norwegian kroner to the Norwegian Officers' Riding Club. Some of this money was used for prizes for a 50 km endurance ride held in 1886, but the legacy still funds prize money, and the Club supported the 80 km ELDRIC ride at Eidskog in 1986, held two years after endurance riding became formally organised under a committee of the Norwegian Equestrian Federation.

Currently there are about 20 endurance rides held in Norway, and most of the riders and organisers live in the south-east between Oslo and Lillehammer. The Nordic Championship was first held in 1989 and in the first five years was won on three occasions by Arabians. Notable amongst the pure-breds competing in the early 1990s was the mare Zubaida (Figaro ex Zela), who with her young rider Ole Kr. Doblong won the Norwegian Junior Championship in 1990 and 1991.

The outstanding rider Reidar Naess is also responsible for much of the endurance riding organisation, and he competed with the mare Saraj (Rajmek ex Saranthe), imported from England, and with her won the 1982 Karoliner Ride in Sweden, before Norwegian endurance riding had officially begun. Saraj was also an excellent dressage performer, and from 1983 to 1986 won the national award for the best Arabian dressage horse. Her son, Sarin, by Ibn Saoud, foaled in 1980, also competed successfully in endurance and was National Champion in 1987.

In 1986 Reidar Naess introduced his Swedish-bred gelding Skamir (Cashmir ex Riscindi) with three short rides. At the age of 12, after eight seasons Skamir had established himself as the top endurance horse in Norway; he was Champion every year from 1988 to 1993; and was also second (in 1989) and twice third (1988 and 1993) in the ELDRIC Trophy list, in addition to representing his country abroad. Another successful year in 1994 gave Skamir the highest points to win the ELDRIC Arab Trophy, following his second place the previous year.

Sweden

Long distance rides were held by the Swedish military around the turn of the century, but the first in modern times was the Karoliner Ride which started in 1977. Commemorating Sweden's King Charles XII and two officers who rode from Pitesci in Turkey to Strahlsund in Germany, a distance of 2,400 km, in 14 days, it is now one of Sweden's three international rides.

Swedish riders owe a great debt of gratitude to Louise Hermelin, a breeder of Arab horses, whose enthusiasm and hard work for the sport has been the force behind endurance riding for nearly two decades. In addition to being an international representative of the Swedish Equestrian Federation, she is also one of their top endurance riders and has represented her country abroad. Her first international horse was a part-bred gelding, Herkules, of 90 per cent Arabian blood, who in the seventh year of his career at the age of 16 in 1983 finished sixth out of 47 starters in one of Europe's toughest rides, the Vienna to Budapest 300 km three day ride. Currently Louise has had great success with her pure-bred Zharek (Zareef ex Langley Magic Hor), who won the Nordic Championship in 1990 and was third in the ELDRIC Arab Trophy in 1994.

Louise Hermelin with her stallion Zharek, Gold Medal winner at the 1990 Nordic Championship.

In 1993 Sweden's best endurance horse was the pure-bred gelding Janos (Gokart ex Janka) belonging to the Nelson family. Janos was bought as a five year old in 1987 and Knut Nelson started competing with him the following year. In 1991, after three successful seasons 14-year-old Catherina took over the ride, having competed for some years on her Welsh pony Musse, and had a brilliant first year with Janos, winning four of their seven rides over distances of 80 to 130 km, including the Nordic Championships over 120 km, which took place in Denmark; and then the oldest Swedish endurance ride, Karoliner, also of 120 km. They were the Swedish

Janos and Catherina Nelson in Sweden.

Champion Horse and Rider (judged on points) and third for the ELDRIC Arab Horse Trophy. Catherina and Janos won four of their seven rides in 1992 and took the Nordic Distance Pokal for the horse with the most kilometres in competition and the best veterinary results.

In 1993 Catherina and Janos won the Swedish Championship and were chosen for the team to represent their country at the European Championships in the U.K. at Southwell. With the support of her family, crewing for her, Catherina rode a superb race to finish second to Egyptian Khalifa, and help towards the Swedish team's award of the Silver medal; in addition Janos became the Swedish Champion horse.

Second to Janos in that year's Swedish Championship was Prince Aussi, ridden by Gun Carlson, who has been taking part in endurance for 12 years and who also enjoys family support. Gun says that she likes the challenge of endurance riding, the feeling of togetherness with her horse, and the opportunity of meeting like-minded people. Aussi, a seven-year-old part-bred Arab, was bred in Australia and brought to Sweden for the 1990 World Equestrian Games at Stockholm. He was acquired by Gun, who won the Swedish Championship with him in 1992, and has several times represented Sweden with him in European and World Championships; in 1993 Gun was third in the ELDRIC Rider Trophy. They came a very creditable twelfth in the World Championship at The Hague.

The Swedish A.H.S. has supported owners of Arabians competing in endurance by sponsoring them in various ways.

Austria

The principal event in Austrian endurance riding is the 300 km Vienna to Budapest ride over three days, which is jointly organised by Austria and Hungary. Held for the first time in 1983 it was won by Dr Hilde Jarc with her Shagya Arab Samum.

Samum was bred in the Styrian Alps and was bought as a four year old by Hilde and Andreas Jarc. Up to the age of 11 he competed successfully in dressage, show-jumping and eventing, but when Hilde Jarc and a group of friends started to organise endurance rides in 1980 his career changed. He had his first international win in a 100 km ride the year before winning the Vienna to Budapest race in a riding time of 18 hours and 40 minutes, two and a half hours ahead of the second horse placed. The following year he was beaten by 30 seconds in the 100 mile Florac in France – but ended his remarkable career in 1985 at the age of 16 by winning Austria's first 100 miler and the Open European Championships, where riders from eight countries were competing.

Germany

The National Association founded in 1976 for Germany and known as Verein Deutscher Distanzreiter e. V. (V.D.D.) was largely responsible for the foundation of ELDRIC. Germany is still one of the leading countries in Europe in endurance riding.

However, the idea of official endurance riding in Germany was started by a group of Arabian breeders. The first ride took place in 1969; it was organised by the Arabian Stud Farm of Schmidt-Ankum and was held in conjunction with an Arabian Stud show. Open to all breeds and over a distance of 50 km it was won in convincing style by Karl-Heinz Ohliger's pure-bred stallion Shraffran (Hadban Enzahi ex Halisa).

In 1974 Herr Winter organised a 100 km ride and this was won by a 20-year-old pure-bred Arabian gelding Firebird, by Shariff out of Tamri, who was bred in England. Firebird belonged to Penelope Dauster who for many years took a leading part in the development of long distance riding, both as secretary to ELDRIC and as a competitor.

Penelope lived in England before her marriage and she rode Firebird in a variety of events before taking him to Germany in 1964. In 1960 he was fourth in the Ridden Mares and Geldings at the A.H.S. National Show and he competed in Small Hack classes and Hunter Trials, as well as being hunted; he also reached the finals of the Riding Clubs' Prix Caprilli. It was not until 1972, at the age of 18, that Firebird started in endurance but his owner soon found that his best form was over long distances and in strong competition – his win over 100 km in 7 hours 17 minutes was a remarkable achievement for a 20 year old after such an energetic life.

During the 1980s Penelope rode two other Arabian geldings from England, Crystal Crown (General D'Orsaz ex Crystal Magic) and Houari (Hari ex Thelma). One of her best years was in 1982 when Crystal Crown won the Swiss Schnabelsberger Cup 100 miler and also the German Championship. Houari also competed abroad and won at Snapphane in Sweden as well as notching up many wins in Germany.

One remarkable endurance 'horse' was Nico, a German Riding Pony by the pure-bred Nabuch out of a half-Arab pony mare, and barely 14 hands high. He was owned by one of Germany's first long distance riders, Lothar Schenzel. They competed regularly at home and abroad in the 1980s and Nico made up for his small size by his distinctive character and very competitive spirit. In 1983 Nico won three Kleinpferd (small horse) divisions over varying distances, including an outright win in the Swiss Schnabelsberg Cup over 100 miles. The following year he was again the overall winner of the 50 mile Herzberger Endurance Ride and the

Schnabelsberg Cup, and also was the outright winner of the Vienna to Budapest 300 km three day ride. A third successive win in the Herzberger followed in 1985, and then the German Championship over 260 km in three days, with a total riding time of 16 hours 12 minutes, in 1986. A truly remarkable record for a mighty atom!

Doris Melzer's black Arabian Al Azim (Elage ex Ramalla) had amassed a total of 5,444 km in endurance rides up to 1995, a record in Germany for a stallion of any breed. In 1993 he won four of his eleven rides and came third in a 160 km qualifier for the 1994 World Championship for which he was nominated. Unfortunately a kick from a visiting mare just before the event prevented him going to the Netherlands; nonetheless he added to his total of completed kilometres during the season, with a win over 100 km, and good placing in ELDRIC rides in Switzerland and Denmark. Al Azim's offspring are now beginning to make their mark as performance horses.

Doris Melzer on her stallion Al Azim, followed by Martina Melzer on the Trakehner, Fatima, 125 km ELDRIC Ride, 1993.

Switzerland

The first endurance rides in Switzerland were held in 1972, and six years later their national association was founded. Switzerland was a founder member of ELDRIC and in 1981 Dr Georg Riedler from Ebikon became its President, a position he held until 1990 when he took over as Secretary and Treasurer for a six-year period.

Dr Riedler was head of two departments at Lucerne Hospital, but despite a very busy schedule he still managed to find time to ride his own horses as well as devoting himself to endurance riding in Europe where his influence has been outstanding.

In the mid 1980s he was the leading distance rider in Switzerland, mostly mounted on his Shagya gelding, Gazal IX-4, who was bred at Babolna, on whom he competed in several international rides, including one of the major long rides, the eight day Madrid to Lisbon 640 km ride in 1987.

Italy

Although organised endurance riding in Italy began in 1968 and the first official ride took place in 1971, the sport did not emerge as a national equestrian discipline as rapidly as in some other countries.

Italian riders were well to the fore in 1993, however, with five rider/horse combinations in the top ten of the ELDRIC competition. In first place was Sergio Tommasi, who also won the Rider Trophy, with his pure-bred mare, 11-year-old Ramegwa Rhodora imported from the U.S.A. in 1993. Her principal win in 1993 came at the Barcelona ride of 200 km over two days; she took the ELDRIC Arab Trophy that year and was second in 1994.

France

Although endurance riding began in a small way in France in 1965, the first major organised ride was not held until 1975 over 130 km at Florac. The winner was Persik (Kankan ex Pamietka) and he won again the following year. Persik, bred in Russia, has proved a remarkably successful sire of endurance horses, his progeny including one ELDRIC and three French champions.

The national governing body for endurance, Le Comité National des Raids Equestre d'Endurance (C.N.R.E.E.) was formed in 1976. Membership grew dramatically and in 1994 had reached the figure of 3,500, with 706 rides organised that year, seven of which were national (130 to 200 km). There were 402 horses of Arabian breeding competing and 33 of them qualified at 'national' level.

One of the earlier riders was Françoise Rimbaud who, with her Arabian gelding Kamir II, began winning awards for her country in 1983. They were members of the Gold Medal winning team in the 1983 European Trophy, followed by a fifth place the following year when the championships were held at Florac; in 1985 they were second in the Swiss William Tell ride and won at Florac. At the World Championship at Rome in 1986 Kamir was the highest-placed French horse, finishing seventh and helping win the Team Bronze medal for France; he finished the season in third place for the ELDRIC Trophy.

First place in the ELDRIC Trophy in 1991 was taken by Relzouck Monepiat, a half-Arab by the Arabian Marzouck out of a Selle Français mare, of part-Thoroughbred and Arab breeding. Ridden by Lise Chambost he competed in and won his first 130 km ride in 1990 at the age of seven. His successes the following year were outstanding, with wins in Switzerland in the 160 km one day William Tell ride at Luzern, at Florac over the same distance, and in Spain in the 198 km two day ride at Barcelona.

Second place in the ELDRIC Trophy that year went to another French horse of Arab breeding, Bernard Daniel's Anglo-Arab Outlaw. He won the William Tell ride in Luzern, was third at L'Ardennoise 120 km ride, and won the European Championships in France.

One of the most consistent and lengthy records, however, is that of Denis Pesce's Melfinik, a son of Persik out of a Selle Français mare. Beginning his winning career in 1985 with a win at Montelimar over 130 km and at Cherveus over the same distance, they continued to win at top level over the next eight years. Their wins included three at Florac, two at Montcuq, and four times they were included in the French team for European and World Championships. In 1987 they won the ELDRIC Trophy and were second in 1993 and in the following year, when they won at Madrid. Their outstanding achievement in 1994, however, was the Silver Medal in the World Championship. The 16-year-old Melfinik fought a tremendous dual for first place with the American Pieraz before being beaten by just under six minutes. Another French rider, Stepháne Fleury with the pure-bred Roch, by Fawzan, won the Bronze Medal, coming in almost nine minutes later.

In addition to competition endurance riding, Arabians have been chosen for epic journeys and long distance rides covering thousands of miles. On their two year 'Trans-Moyen Orient' Ride, which began in 1982, two French riders, Jean-Claude Cazade and Pascale Francone, rode the young Arabian stallions El Merindian and El Mzuina, half-brothers bred at M. Josain Valette's Haras de Gardelle, by Al Drif and out of Indian Firebird and Velvet Night, two mares from England.

French rider Denis Pesce and Melfinik at the 1994 World Equestrian Games at The Hague.

The aim of the ride was to try to beat the long distance riding record held by Tschiffely of 16,093 km from Buenos Aires to New York in 504 days. A year was spent breaking and training the two youngsters, planning the ride and dealing with documents to enable the riders to travel through several countries around the Mediterranean.

Their route took them through Italy, Yugoslavia, Greece, Turkey, Syria and Jordan to their goal, Saudi Arabia, and back again to France. Delays waiting for visas and other government regulations when making their way through the Middle East led to many lost days and the journey took them two years and two months. However, by riding 21,070 km they broke the record.

Arriving back to an enthusiastic reception in Paris with their horses in superb condition, Pascale and Jean-Claude were most generously given their two mounts by M. Valette. His dream had been fulfilled – with careful breeding and training two of his stallions had proved to the world that his Arabians were just as tough as their ancestors.

U.S.A.

Challenging, breathtaking and historic, the Western States 100 Mile Ride, popularly known as the Tevis Cup, is undoubtedly the most famous endurance ride in the world. It was the brainchild of Wendell Robie, Auburn banker and landowner who was responsible for the conservation of the spectacular old trail first used by the Washoe Indians and later by miners travelling between the silver mines of Nevada and the goldfields of California.

Wishing to find out if present-day horses could match the achievements of the mounts of the famous Wells Fargo and Pony Express riders of the previous century over the same trail, Wendell Robie inaugurated the race in 1955 and it has been held annually since. He rode it himself 13 times, winning on four occasions. His mounts included the Arabian stallion Bandos (Nasr ex Baida) on whom he won the first two events, and his son Siri, who won the Best Condition Award. Bandos also sired numerous other successful endurance horses.

The Ride begins at Squaw Valley, a ski resort at 6,200 feet in Nevada, and competitors traverse the magnificent Sierra mountain range by way of Emigrants Pass (8,750 ft) down to Auburn (7,495 ft) in California – a wilderness trail described as 'not something for the faint of heart'.

Its prestigious awards commemorate the historical gold rush background of the event, with the winner holding the perpetual Trophy, the Tevis Cup, donated by Lloyd Tevis, former President of the Wells Fargo Company, whilst the Haggin Cup for the Best Conditioned horse was presented by James B. Haggin, pioneer and friend of Lloyd Tevis and an eminent breeder of top-class horses. The completion award for all those who finish the Ride within the 24-hour time limit is the much coveted splendid silver buckle, engraved with a Pony Express rider and the name of the ride.

Not only has the Tevis Cup Ride given ample proof that today's horses are just as tough as their counterparts of earlier days, but in addition its strict rules came to be used as a guideline by other countries organising their own national 100 mile events. Wendell Robie's dedication to endurance riding has had far reaching results, for as well as pioneering the Tevis Cup and giving generous and practical support, he also bred and trained horses which he loaned out so other riders could achieve success. His outstanding contribution to the sport put the U.S.A. in the forefront of those countries which have most influenced endurance riding.

A list of winners of the Tevis Cup shows that in 40 years only three horses were not of Arabian breeding. The vast majority have been pure-bred and the remainder half to seven-eighths Arabian.

Not everyone who enters the Tevis Cup intends to ride competitively – just to finish is a big challenge in itself. Young riders often compete with a parent and in 1994 Wendell Robie's great-grandson, Wendell Arnold, rode with his mother, Marion, who had won in 1969 on the pure-bred mare, Hailla (Bandos ex Canastilla). Hailla, by then aged 34, was present at the ceremonies held to mark the fortieth year of the event.

Appropriately, in celebration of the fortieth anniversary, there was an impressive list of previous winning riders and Top Ten horses in the field of 202 competitors, 115 of whom finished. Winner for the second consecutive year was Chris Knoch with NV Fifth Avenue (Bey Shah ex Pennie Lane). The Haggin Cup is just as much coveted as the Tevis and the qualifiers are the first ten horses to finish which have carried 165 pounds or more. The panel of 15 vets were unanimous in giving the award to Sandy Schuler's WCM Magnet (Magyar ex JLR Shana) who finished third 100 minutes after the winner but carrying over 200 pounds; he had also won the previous year, finishing eighth.

The Tevis Cup Ride was not, however, the first organised endurance event to be run in America. At around the time that the A.H.S. held their Tests in Sussex, the U.S. Army were organising endurance rides of 300 miles ridden in five days as tests for cavalry horses. Two of these were won by British-bred Arabians, the mare Ramla (Astraled ex Ridaa) which carried 14½ stone in 1919 and the gelding, Crabbet (Rijm ex Narda), winning in 1921 and, it is claimed, in doing so achieving a world record for speed and weight carried in a race of that distance. Crabbet was carrying 17½ stone, an

Mother and daughter on the trail. Rebecca Moss on D-Sha-Raz and her mother, Juliet, riding Sahara Ace in the 1986 Tevis Cup.

outstanding example of the Arabian's strength for its size. A third Arabian of British breeding, the 14.2 hh mare Noam, a full sister to Crabbet, finished the 1920 ride while carrying nearly a third of her 825 pounds' weight. The only stallion of any breed to finish one of the rides was the pure-bred El Sabok (El Jafil ex Narkeesa) who came in first but was disqualified for a welt on his back. The convincing superiority of the Arabians over other breeds in these rides was a contributory factor to the decision of the U.S. Army to bring in Arabian stallions for breeding Cavalry remounts.

During the Second World War a little chestnut gelding, El Azhar, emerged as a superb endurance horse at the age of 15. Having had several homes up until then, during which time he had been trained as an exhibition jumper over novelty obstacles ranging from kitchen chairs to blazing bars, he competed in a 100 mile ride in 1939 and came fourth. Over the next four years El Azhar had three firsts and two seconds (one in a 75 miler). In one of his last rides, when neither he nor his owner, Harry McGlothlen, were absolutely fit, he finished first at a Des Moines 100 miler but was relegated to second place when the judges considered him tired after cooling down – he was then nearly 20 years old! In between endurance rides, El Azhar was winning prizes in three-gaited pleasure and pair classes.

Another early partnership was that of Linda Tellington, well-known author and teacher who devised the Tellington Touch technique of training, and her tough little mare Bint Gulida (Ghadaf ex Gulida). They pioneered the concept of competing in more than one 100 miler in a year. On one occasion they rode over the trail of the Tevis Cup a few days before the Ride and then in the Ride itself finished sixth, without Bint Gulida being pushed at all, and six weeks later won the Jim Shoulders Ride in Oklahoma by five and a half hours. Bint Gulida produced a well-known endurance horse and sire, Cougar Rock, by the endurance winner, Bezatal.

For over 40 years Mrs Bazy Tankersley of Al-Marah Arabians has been breeding horses which have had notable success in endurance riding. Mrs Tankersley herself rode Al-Marah Rud Balik (Indraff ex Raab) to win the heavyweight Championship Trophy in the 100 mile Vermont Endurance Ride in 1963 and 1964. Another early rider, the late Tish Hewitt, had the mare Al-Marah Rapturous (Rapture ex Radeyra) who, in addition to winning the Florida 100 mile ride during one show season, was also Canadian Top Ten, a regional reserve champion and a U.S. Top Ten in English Pleasure. In more recent years Al-Mara Xanthyium (Count Rafla ex Expectation) tied for first place in the Tevis Cup in 1992 and is now

Al-Marah Xanthyium negotiating Cougar Rock, Tevis Cup, U.S.A., 1992.

competing with Becky Hart, whilst Al-Marah Tamarind (Count Rafla ex Al-Marah Canadian Peak) has had 25 Top Ten awards out of 32 starts and 9 Best Condition awards; in 1993 he was ranked fourth overall.

Covering a period of over 30 years the Fitzgerald family, husband and wife Pat and Donna and son Mike, have achieved great success with a string of brilliant horses, mostly pure or part-bred Arabians. Outstanding amongst them is the little pure-bred gelding Witezarif (Witezar ex Razifa) who came to the Fitzgerald ranch as a five year old to be sold on. His potential was soon discovered and he was finally purchased by the Fitzgeralds and became Donna's firm partner. Witezarif's three wins in 1970 included his first Tevis Cup Ride, which he proceeded to win on five further occasions and once finished second, an unbroken record to date. He completed 75 rides in all, 26 of them being 100 milers, and was first past the post on 19 occasions. At 24 years of age he had accumulated a total of 5,000 successful competition miles, and was still going strong!

In 1987 Trilby Pederson, a 53-year-old grandmother, and her Arabian gelding Rushcreek won their National Championship an entirely different way, and emphasised the belief that 'to win is to complete'. During the year they competed in 74 endurance rides, completing all but one. They travelled 4,260 miles in competitions, and tens of thousands of miles in the horse trailer, once completing 2,500 miles away from home. Although Rushcreek did not win a single ride he was A.E.R.C. National Champion and finished the season completely sound. Trilby Pederson's policy of never risking her horse for a chance win not only produced the most points and enabled her to win the supreme award but also gave a new concept to the sport in the U.S.A., demonstrating that miles covered can be just as effective (and to some more enjoyable) than simply winning for the sake of winning.

U.S. riders and horses in international competition

The first World Championship, held in Italy in 1986, was won by an Arabian gelding, Omar, owned by Claude Pacheco and ridden by Cassandra Schuler, both of whom are veterinary surgeons. Omar was brought carefully to his peak through eight years of steady training, gradually rising to tackle the top 100 milers including the Purina Race of Champions, in which only the top ranked 100 mile endurance horses can compete. When winning the individual Gold Medal for the U.S.A. in Rome he completed the course in 10 hours, 50 minutes, 30 seconds, finishing half an hour ahead of the next three horses.

Two years later the second World Championships were held in the

U.S.A. and the winner was again a pure-bred, the brilliant 14.3 hh gelding RO Grand Sultan; he finished six minutes ahead of John Crandall riding another Arabian gelding, GT Grisha. RO Grand Sultan is one of the greatest endurance horses of all time. He began his career in 1983 when a five year old and his owner Becky Hart very soon discovered he had a mind of his own – he liked to get on with the job at speed and there were several battles for control, with a few frightening trail experiences, before he settled down. His first competition was over 70 miles – Becky felt that 50 miles was not long enough for the exuberant Sultan! The next year they won their first Tevis Cup; this was followed by the A.E.R.C. National Championship, the North American Endurance Champion Gold Medal and Best Condition award, leading up to a second Tevis Cup win and the World Championship in 1988. Confirming his status as World Champion, Sultan took the individual Gold Medal again in the World Equestrian Games in Sweden in 1990 and then successfully defended his title in Spain in 1992. In 1993, at the age of 16, Sultan showed he was still at the top when winning the North American Endurance Championship (N.A.E.C.) which was held near Calgary over the eastern slopes of the Canadian Rockies, and he also won the coveted Best Condition award.

The tenth Annual Race of Champions, held in 1993 over 100 miles in the Black Hills of South Dakota, the area made famous through *Dances With Wolves*, is a typical example of the dominance of Arabians in endurance riding. There were 105 elite endurance horses entered and riders from the U.S.A. and Canada, with one international team representing Germany, Greece and Australia endeavouring to claim the Champion of Champions title, and the first eight horses to finish were all of Arabian breeding. The winner was Melissa Crain with a freeze-branded but unregistered Arabian gelding who was originally sold in an auction and then exchanged for two young horses and finally purchased by his present owner in 1992 after winning the 1991 National 100 Mile Championship. Second was a half-Arabian, Nugget, and the next six were all pure-breds.

A description of the 1994 World Championships held in the Netherlands was given above, but in enlargement it is interesting to note how Valerie Kanavy trained her pure-bred Pieraz (Pierscien ex Aziella) for his brilliant win.

Taking expert advice she planned a thorough preparation both for herself and her horse and began a fitness programme the previous year. She had flown to the Netherlands with her husband to examine the course, 18 miles of which was through deep sand, and realised that special training would be necessary for this type of going. 'Sand is pretty dead and a horse is required to lift his legs . . . Muscles have to be prepared to do that job or risk injury.'

The mountainous and rocky Virginian countryside where the Kanavys live being totally unlike the terrain around The Hague, Valerie had to innovate and deep snow that winter proved 'a gift from God' for Pieraz's training: 'What better way to condition for sand than deep snow', she wrote.

In February 1994 to test the snow/sand theory they went to Florida for a 100 mile ride over a sandy course and won, beating the course record by two hours and finishing one and a half hours ahead of the next competitor. After that a race-track 45 miles from their home provided the closest surface to sand she could find. Their next ride was the Spring Challenge where they won again and set a new course record and also took the Best Condition award. A second demonstration ride of 100 miles (part of the selection process for the 28 horses nominated for the World Championship) in Mississipi was also won, and two months before the Championships, when the list of six to represent the U.S.A. was announced, the pair was included.

Pieraz was bought as a six year old in 1988 and was brought on slowly. Up to 1992 he had finished in the top ten of several 100 mile rides and that year won the South Carolina 100, this time with Valerie's daughter Danielle riding; he was third in the 1993 Race of Champions in South Dakota, and got the Best Condition.

Pieraz's 1994 World Gold Medal, together with the coveted Best Condition award, at the age of 12, was a testimony to the thorough training programme. Valerie Kanavy believes that whilst heart and lungs can be developed in a comparatively short time, it takes several years to strengthen the rest of the body. This theory is certainly borne out by an analysis of the age at which endurance horses appear to be in their prime.

Canada

Endurance and Competitive Trail riding has been steadily gaining in popularity since the 1960s, but it was not until 1983 that the Canadian Long Distance Riding Association (C.A.L.D.R.A.) was formed.

Competitive trail riding differs from endurance in various respects and is run under the N.A.T.R.C. (covering the whole of North America) which was formed in 1961. Riders are sorted into divisions on a basis of experience and weight (saddle, rider and horse); they go 30 or 50 miles within a certain time period and the route must be completed with 30 minutes leeway – slower detracts from the competition and faster is too hard on the horse. There is a 45 minute mandatory stop for lunch and two veterinary checks, which are usually at unspecified places to ensure an element of surprise for competitors. Riders are also observed (sometimes without their knowledge) and are not allowed to lead their horse at any stage of the ride. Horses are judged on soundness, condition, manners and way of going; riders for horsemanship skills, safe riding practices, trail courtesy and safe camp environment. Horses are checked the evening before the ride, and riders must tend their horse themselves. A judging card given after the ride tells every competitor how they were right or wrong in each category. Trail riding is an excellent way to learn proper methods of training, conditioning and caring for horses and it encourages good horsemanship; those taking part particularly enjoy the friendly and open atmosphere with everyone helping each other.

A successful competitor in the early days was Ruth Kitchen from Ontario with her pure-bred gelding Barra Djadah. In 1969 and 1970 he won the 100 mile Competitive Trail Ride in Vermont, organised by the Green Mountain Horse Association. Ten days after his first win he took part in a one-day event, coming first in cross country and stadium jumping and fourth in dressage.

A very early endurance race in Yukon was won by Victory Candida. Her sire Royal Victory and grandsire Victory Day II were well known in British Columbia for the success of their progeny in a wide variety of ridden events, and as winners of many versatility awards.

In 1985 Danny Grant bought the pure-bred CDR Soliloquy, who had already shown great promise in endurance rides, with the intention of competing with him in Ride and Tie races. After one win and three seconds in 1986, all with Best Condition awards, Danny was invited to join the Canadian team for the first North American Endurance Championship. They were placed eighth and gave Canada her first official international success since C.A.L.D.R.A.'s formation.

In 1993 the North American Endurance Championship was held near Calgary. Over 100 miles of spectacular but difficult terrain on the eastern slopes of the Canadian Rockies, teams from five U.S. and two Canadian regions competed, together with two individual competitors representing Denmark and Switzerland. For the first time in these Championships all the team members in each medal-winning team completed. Included in the Bronze Medal winning Canada East team was Earle Baxter with his pure-bred gelding Rushcreek Pawnee, who has completed five F.E.I. events and has over 3,000 career miles to his credit.

Australia

Endurance riding in Australia is said to have begun as a bushman's sport. It now attracts people from many walks of life and is one of the most rapidly growing equestrian challenges.

However, perhaps partly because to some participants endurance riding in Australia has grown so quickly and has become highly competitive, in the early 1990s the administrators of the sport reviewed and tightened up riding rules after a certain amount of adverse publicity involving accusations of abuse to horses. These rules, made by the Australian Endurance Riders Association (A.E.R.A.), are now amongst the toughest in the world, and vetting standards are more stringent than those in most other countries. An important new rule means that horses and riders new to the sport are categorised as novices to ensure gradual initiation into endurance competition.

In addition to the tightening up of veterinary control during rides, leading veterinary researchers have also contributed much to the monitoring of fitness in horses both in training and competition. Sophisticated veterinary evaluations with various parameters enable the vets to gain a comprehensive picture of how a horse is functioning during a particular ride. These evaluations are not only a guide in regard to the horse's fitness to continue on the trail, but also give riders in-depth knowledge of how their horse reacts under the stress of a stiff endurance test. They are also useful in predicting endurance potential in individual animals. As has already been stated, outstanding endurance performance involves many factors – heart size, muscle physiology, effective respiratory function, conformation, temperament – as well as training, and all these elements have been well explained in articles and instruction in Australia, which is now one of the leading countries in this field.

In the 1994 Quilty Ride blood was taken from a number of horses at the vet checks during the ride in order to conduct further research by relating back to the metabolics and pulse rates of these horses as they were recorded during the ride.

The Quilty Cup

The Quilty Cup 160 km ride is to Australians what the Tevis Cup is to Americans, and it could be said that endurance riding as known today began with the first Ride, held over rugged country in an area west of Sydney in 1966.

According to one version of the Quilty's genesis, quoted by Ann Hyland, it was a chance remark made at a meeting of the Arab Horse Society in Sydney to the effect that 'it was a pity the public were not made aware of the fact that Australian horses must rank among the world's best' which triggered off the concept of the now famous Ride.

Another version is that two men got into conversation and one recounted the days of his youth when nothing was thought of riding 100 miles in a day. He considered there were horses around which were capable of being much more than just 'show ponies' and it was time they were given a chance to reveal their real ability. The two men agreed that one should supply the money and the other provide the track, and a meeting would be called to assemble enthusiastic riders.

It was the famous horseman Tom Quilty, a well-known bushman from Kimberley in Western Australia, who gave the handsome gold cup and his name to the Ride, which has been run ever since with the exploits of the bygone bushmen held always in mind.

Val and Ron Males worked hard to arrange the course for the first ride which was held with veterinary safeguards and close monitering by the R.S.P.C.A. as was done at the first Tevis Cup.

Ben Males (Ron Males' grandson) riding Vivien at Mudgee, Australia, 1994.

The winner of this first Ride, Gabriel Stetcher with his Arabian stallion Shalawi (Shafreyn ex Helawi), not only set a world record of 11 hours 24 minutes actual racing time, but also did it in unique fashion, for he rode bareback most of the time and, being a marathon runner, ran beside his horse for much of the distance.

Ron Males was also one of the competitors to finish, coming fifth on another pure-bred stallion, 11-year-old Shareym, bred similarly to the winner, being by Shafreyn out of the Rakib daughter Ruheym. Six weeks later Shareym was senior champion stallion at the National Stud Horse and Pony Show. Shareym was a real family horse and during the next eight years he initiated the Males' young son and daughter to the Quilty – juniors can ride in it at 15 years of age.

Nearly 30 years later Ron is still actively involved with endurance riding. In 1993 he rode Palexis (Milex ex Promissa) to win his twelfth Quilty Completion Buckle, a coveted award, and the following year he was in the Middle East advising on the training of Arabians sold through him to the Royal Stud in Abu Dhabi, two of which finished second and third (this was Palexis) in a 'Horse versus Camel' marathon in Qatar. Ron won his thirteenth Quilty Buckle riding Ralvon Sunflower in 1994.

Glenallon Solomon, a part-bred by Diablo out of Bulliluna, ridden by Jenny Oliver, had the distinction of becoming the first horse to win three successive Quilty Rides, in 1985 to 1987. The winner in 1991 and 1992 was Andrew Bailey's pure-bred Tantawanglo Hamal Zahab, by Sky Hussar.

The Quilty is now the National Championship Ride and it has been completely dominated by Arabians, Anglos and part-breds. In the three years from 1991 their record has been as follows: in 1991 of the Top Ten place winners in the four divisions (heavyweight, middleweight, lightweight and junior), 20 were pure-breds and 13 of Arab breeding, with the winners of each section being pure-bred; in 1992 of the Top Tens in heavyweight, middleweight and lightweight and top five junior, only one, a palomino Quarter Horse, was not of Arab breeding; in 1993 all but two of the Top Ten in the senior division were of Arab breeding, as were all three of the finishers. In fact, during the 28 years it has been held the Quilty Cup has only once been won by a horse with no Arabian blood, and five of the winners have been pure-bred.

The 1993 Quilty was held in Tasmania in some of the worst weather ever known for the Ride, with blizzards on the day itself. When the 116 starters set off at midnight it was still snowing and by 3 a.m. it had deteriorated even further. Conditions were so hazardous that the third leg of the course, over a steep mountain spur, was pronounced too dangerous and a last minute change of course had to be made, though it did stop snowing later. Fifty-five horses completed and passed the final vetting and the winner of the Quilty Cup was a part-bred mare, Sharahd Caprice (Flambeau ex Cornice), owned and ridden by Bob Sample. Despite such difficult conditions Sharahd Caprice won in 10 hours 23 minutes carrying 89.2 kg, and she also took the Best Conditioned award in her middleweight division.

Caprice was bred specially for this kind of work at Bob Sample's Sharahd Stud, which was founded with the offspring of two Arabian stallions, Flambeau (Sindh ex Falusaf) and Tallangatta Muftakher (Royal Domino ex Iole). His aim is to produce part-breds with a high percentage of Arabian blood, and two Quilty winners and many other exceptional endurance horses have been bred at Sharahd.

For various reasons not all junior riders continue with the sport as seniors but a notable exception is Brook Sample, who at the age of 12 chose one of his father's foals as his future mount. In 1990, in his first attempt as a senior, Brook won the Quilty Cup and in 1993 riding the Anglo-Arab Sharahd Cavalier he and his father finished together. Brook's horse unfortunately vetted out lame and so his father won. The following year Brook was eighth in the World Equestrian Games at The Hague.

The Shahzada

Described as one of the longest annual Marathons in the world, the Shahzada 400 km ride was first held in 1981. It is named in commemoration

of the British-born Arabian stallion, winner of two 300 mile endurance tests in England in 1920 and 1922, who was exported in 1925. Shahzada was valued very highly in Australia and his name appears in the pedigrees of many of today's endurance horses. The event is modelled on the early British and American cavalry horse tests, and competitors cover 50 miles each day for five days.

The aim in the Shahzada Memorial Endurance Test as stressed by the organising committee is not simply to win but to cross the finishing line and present an unstressed and healthy horse to the vets half an hour later and be

Brook Sample on Sharahd Cavalier and his father, Bob, riding Sharahd Caprice, 200 yards from the finish of the 1993 Quilty Ride in Tasmania.

The start of the 1920 Arab Horse Society Endurance Test At Lewes. The grey Shahzada and, on right, Robin, first and second.

judged fit to continue. In fact, the motto of the A.E.R.A. is 'To complete is to win.'

As with the Quilty, only qualified endurance horses and riders are allowed to start, and once again Arabians and part-breds dominate the event. During the 13 years it had been held up to 1993, with one exception, the fastest times have been made by five pure-breds and five part-breds, one of which won three times. The Best Managed and Best Conditioned horses have been entirely of Arabian breeding, with the exception of one mule, Juanita, who completed successfully in the first Ride and again in 1983 and 1984.

The best time in the 1993 Test was that of Geoff Hurt's pure-bred gelding Kejome Komet (Halal ex Larabon Aneeka) in 28 hours 53 minutes. However, Geoff Hurt's comment afterwards sums up the ideals of this event:

Just getting through the week is what it is all about. To know that you can go out twice a day for five days and at the end of it have a fit horse, that is really the elation of the Shahzada. Winning is nice, but that is not what it is all about. Shahzada is about completing and having a good horse at the end of the day.

One of the most prestigious achievements in endurance riding in Australia is to hold both Shahzada and Quilty Buckles. Amongst the record holders of this achievement the part-bred Andarra Shareef (Shareym ex Mercury) has won five Quilty and two Shahzada Buckles; another part-bred, Gilellad, holds six Shahzada and three Quilty; the pure-bred gelding Cedar Ridge Rob Roy (Flash Design ex Stoodleigh Nikia) has a good record spanning six years, with four Quilty and two Shahzada Buckles, and in 1987 and 1992 he also returned the fastest time. Other multiple holders include Merrivale Voss (Arab/Welsh Mountain) and the pure-bred stallion Oasis Desert Song (Abyad ex Caithness Walzaway) with three Quilty and two Shahzada.

There are, of course, numerous other major rides as well as countless smaller ones for initiating beginners. During the 1980s Terry Wood's Anglo-Arab Andarra Shareef was accumulating wins, and Top Tens, together with

Down the steps at the 1993 Shahzada in Australia: Rachael Bohn with Silver Ibn Zarak, winner of eight buckles.

a large number of Best Condition awards; in 1983 and 1984 he was National Horse of the Year. Still going strong in 1992 at the age of 18 he successfully completed the Shahzada, and in 1994 completed a 100 km ride.

The Anglo-Arab Balfour Marbella commenced her career at the age of seven and her many wins include two in the lightweight division of the Quilty in 1982 and 1983; at the age of 20 and ridden by her owners' 12-year-old daughter Bronwyn Knight-Rutland she successfully completed her last ride with heart recoveries of 39, 39!

Australia has a fine record in international endurance. June Petersen was the only Australian to take home a medal from the 1990 Equestrian Games when with Wertaloona Lionel she won the Bronze. In the 1994 Games the Australians who took the team Bronze Medal were all mounted on purebreds. Christine Forrester rode the gelding Mandala Galactic (Gaspar ex Gisela) to finish equal seventeenth and a few seconds behind her came Melonie De Jong riding another gelding, Vet School Laurence (Vet School Mollonqbar ex Vet School Madam) in twentieth place. The third member of the team, Barbara Timms, came in just over six minutes later on the mare

BELOW LEFT *Wilma Roache at the 1993 Shahzada riding Ky, a brumby she caught as a foal in the Snowy Mountains.*

BELOW RIGHT *Junior rider Bronwyn Knight on Valinor Park Armistice, followed by Tristan Knight with Valinor Park Liberty.*

Kildara Sharina (Afandi ex Pasadena Natasha). The Australians were only six minutes behind the Spanish who, in fact, overtook them on the final few kilometres through The Hague. They took a risk hand-galloping through the streets, but the gamble paid off and they took the Silver Medal. The Spanish team consisted of one pure-bred and three Anglo-Arabs.

New Zealand

The first recorded endurance ride in New Zealand took place on 29 August 1970. It was run by a well-known Arabian breeder, Jack Evans, with assistance from Tokoroa Pony Club, and was held over 50 miles, with 22 competitors taking part. A year later the New Zealand Committee of the Australasian Arab Horse Society organised the first 100 mile one day ride. Fifteen horses competed and seven finished, one of which was the Arabian mare Silver Fern (Meladdin [Imp.] ex Semna [Imp.]) who was in foal at the time and some months later produced a strong, healthy foal.

During the 1970s a few intrepid riders travelled to Australia to compete in the Quilty Ride and to the U.S.A. to observe the Tevis Cup Ride. Their enthusiasm helped to promote interest in the sport and gradually groups of people formed clubs and horse organisations to run rides throughout the North and South Islands. Rules were based on Australian regulations but tended to vary from club to club; this caused considerable confusion to riders, and so eventually agreement was reached concerning the formation of the National Endurance Society.

The first meeting was held in 1975 and a steering committee was set up with the aim of establishing a standard set of rules. In 1976 a further meeting took place to inaugurate a permanent New Zealand Association; but three years later it was discovered that this Association had never been correctly registered as an Incorporated Society. So it was not until 1981 at a General Meeting that the fully incorporated New Zealand Endurance and Trail Rides Association (N.Z.E.T.R.) came into being. Membership is mostly through affiliated clubs which run the many rides now held. These consist of Endurance Rides, beginning with short training rides of 10 km; 'fun treks' up to 40 km; and the longer rides of 80 to 160 km. For these longer events horses must not be less than five years old; competitors start together and the winner is the first horse to cross the line and be judged in fit condition, theoretically, to continue.

Competitive Trail Rides can be held over the same course as the Endurance Rides, but a time limit is operated and points are lost for finishing before or after the limit. Riders start at intervals and the vetting is similar to Endurance Rides; the heart rate must return to 60 beats per

Joy Redshaw riding Kadin and (behind) Kalee Coster on Nellie Boswell during the Taumarunie 160 km ride in New Zealand, 1993. Mt Ruapehu is in the background.

minute or less and lameness results in elimination. Penalty points are incurred for lost shoes, saddlery rubs and interference. The winner is the horse which qualifies closest to the time specified, and who has the best recovery heart rate and least number of penalty points.

One exceptional endurance horse of the earlier period was the 14.2 hh Arabian gelding Waimeha Whirlwind, by Grey Swirl out of Waimeha Alison, owned by Joe Pittams. He won 14 consecutive 50 mile rides in a three-year period and the 1978 Nationals, after which he was presented with the McGregor Rose Bowl for his achievements. Described as a 'versatile Arabian in the true sense of the word', he became a show-jumper after his endurance career and won many competitions, including the prestigious Isola Pony Derby in 1985. Whirlwind also won in the show-ring and was a champion under saddle before going on to eventing, at which he excelled, and was in the Area Trials team at Palmerston North. In retirement in 1992 his legs, despite all their work, were described as completely clean with not a mark on them.

New Zealand's first international winner was another from Waimeha, the late Alan Sisam's stud – 'where it all began', as one writer referred to the start of Arab horse breeding in New Zealand. This was Ray Tylee's Waimeha Enterprise by the great performance sire Dynamit out of Frazil Freda. Together with Andrea Mason's part-bred Ambrose, and Mannie Gall with Nellie Boswell (an Anglo-Arab by the Arabian Impetuous out of the Thoroughbred mare Blonde Fury), they formed the first New Zealand team to travel to Australia to take part in the Quilty Endurance Ride of 1991. Ambrose, who had won several major titles, and Nellie Boswell were unfortunately vetted out over the tough course, but Waimeha Enterprise won the Heavyweight Division. Two years later Nellie Boswell, ridden by 15-year-old Kalee Coster, took the North Island Junior Championship in 1993.

Other Waimeha horses to create records include the stallion Waimeha Mandate (Dynamit ex Waimeha Muna) owned by Noel Ritchie, who became the first Arabian to qualify in over 3,000 km of endurance riding and by 1994 had achieved 6,000 km. Two bad accidents, when on each occasion a bridge gave way under him during a ride causing severe injuries to his hind legs, left Mandate undaunted. Joint winner of the 1992 North Island Championship, he qualified in over 43 rides and only twice in his career has he failed the vet check due to his heart rate. Mandate was Open

Noel Ritchie and Waimeha Mandate in the Te Kauwhata region of New Zealand, 1994.

Distance Horse of the Year in 1992 and for the second successive year finished second in 1993 in the Tasman Forestry Open National Endurance Championship Ride of 200 miles over two days.

Mannie Gall's Anglo-Arab gelding Mohammed Ali was the first New Zealand horse to complete 3,000 km. In 1987 Mannie Gall, who became President of N.Z.E.T.R. in 1984, won the National Championship with Mohammed Ali and together they became that year's 'Horse and Rider of the Year'. Mohammed Ali was a boisterous character, and in his early days disliked being disciplined, but his behaviour gradually improved through his work as a shepherd's hack. His owner described him as a true work horse, and attributes much of his success to mustering cattle over hilly rough country, and long slow training for endurance, because Mohammed Ali had the disadvantage of a very high heart rate, compared to most pure-breds.

The horse who beat Waimeha Mandate in the 1992 and 1993 Tasman Forestry National Championship Ride was Zephyr, a part-bred Arab owned by Paulette Stannard, by the pure-bred Ngapa Joussif out of a stockhorse mare; they thus became the first ever combination to win the National Championship for two consecutive years, as well as the Best Conditioned Horse Award. Paulette is the top rider of her country and a superb horsewoman; being a slight person she has to carry several kilograms of lead as deadweight.

The year 1993 was a great one for Zephyr, who achieved over 1,000 km with five wins; a second and a third; and five fittest horse awards. He was also Distance Horse of the Year and North Island Champion, and finally he and Paulette were Horse and Rider of the Year. By 1994 Zephyr had over 4,000 qualified km, a total of 12 wins and 14 Best Conditioned Horse awards; that year he was once again New Zealand National Champion and Best Conditioned, over 160 km, and North Island Champion over 120 km, and Best Condition.

Endurance riding is developing rapidly in New Zealand and the incidence of the success of Arabians and their derivatives is just as marked as it is in every country.

South Africa

Endurance riding in South Africa had its beginnings in 1964 when letters published in the *Landbouweekblad* (the Afrikaans farmers' weekly magazine) throughout that year deliberated 'which breed was the toughest and capable of the greatest endurance?' The controversy aroused such interest that in December the *Landbouweekblad* announced that a Marathon Horse Race was to be organised on 29 March 1965, and rules were made and published.

The magazine carried numerous articles about the horses and the enthusiasm of would-be competitors, and disputation over the merits of different breeds continued in the letters columns.

This March ride, however, was preceded by one held on 16 February of the same year. The 126 mile route lay from George over the Outiniqua Mountains. It was reported that only three of the twelve competitors finished the ride and two horses died, which caused an outcry; it was realised that both horse and rider needed to be extremely fit for such an arduous undertaking.

The Landbouweekblad Ride was entirely different. It was held on two days over 104 miles between Hanover, De Aar and Richmond, and according to the *Volksblad* only 69 of the 144 starters were allowed to continue, which suggests proper veterinary supervision. The winner was Boet Ferreira of the Eastern Cape, riding a 'pure-bred flea-bitten grey Arabian mare' named Lorraine, though her exact breeding is not known. The third and fourth placed horses were also said to be 'flea-bitten greys'. Presumably this settled the argument over which breed was best suited for endurance, but as no official records of the horses' breeding existed it is not possible to be more detailed. Nevertheless, Arabian horse breeders were delighted with the publicity their favourites were attracting.

These marathons were the forerunners for well-organised and highly successful South African endurance rides and various pre-rides that developed in the 1970s. The beautiful African scenery, with its vast plains and spectacular mountains and valleys, provides added incentive for riders to take on longer than ordinary pleasure rides. The popularity grew rapidly after the Endurance Ride Association of South Africa (E.R.A.S.A.) was founded in 1974. Professors S. van Heerden and Littlejohn, as well as a veterinary panel from Onderstepoort, were all involved, and much scientific data was recorded.

The National Championship takes place each year at Fauresmith, in the southern Free State, and the course, originally 210 km but now 200, is ridden over three days. To qualify for the Championship a rider–horse combination has to complete at least three pre-rides of 80 km or longer in the six months preceding the Championship. Veterinary supervision is very strict and after each ride the best conditioned horse is nominated by the veterinary panel.

A special feature of the 1980 National Endurance Ride was the presence of a well-equipped physiology laboratory, staffed by fully trained technicians and veterinarians, where blood samples of competing horses could be analysed on the spot. It was said to be the first time such a facility had been made available to endurance riders during a competition.

Veterinary check.

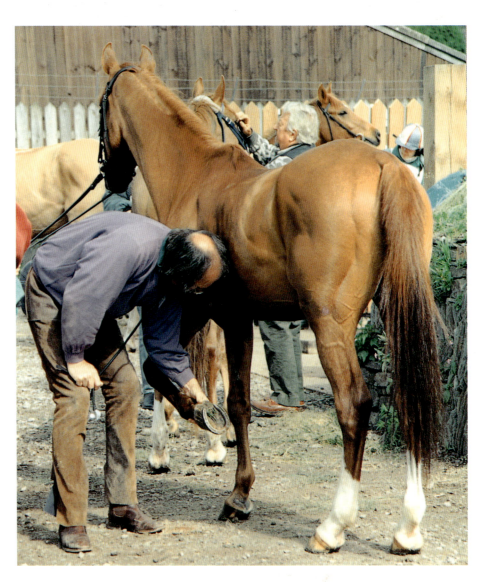

A breakdown of the 20 fastest horses in the 1990 National Championship showed that seven were pure-bred Arabians, six part-bred and five Anglo-Arabs; the remaining two were a Thoroughbred/Boerperd and a cross-bred.

Amongst early successful Arabians in endurance was Marielotte Klugkist's Eibna Nasletta (Vlinkfontein Nasser ex Eibna Albileta). Ridden by Angus Strover, in 1976 he won the 210 km Arabian Horse Endurance Ride in 13 hours 8 minutes; previous to this he had achieved great success in the show-ring.

A remarkable achievement was that of Mrs E. de Vos in 1982 who, at the age of 66, broke the existing record to win in 8 hours, 37 minutes on the pure-bred Nourmahal Mustapha (Queensway Shadow Play ex Timarie Lady Mae). Mrs de Vos and Nourmahal Mustapha were still competing in 1985

LEFT *Final vetting, and* BELOW
crewing on ride.

and again won the trophy for the most senior rider completing the 210 km. In 1992 a new record was made when Jennifer Reed completed the course in 8 hours, 13 minutes and 40 seconds on Belthazar Flinkfontein.

Nourmahal Mustapha has an exceptional record in several disciplines as well as in the show-ring. He has been awarded three legions of merit for endurance riding and racing, and one for showing under saddle. In addition he has been successful in dressage, eventing and cross country. Now retired to stud, his progeny are winning in the show-ring and in endurance.

With around 1,300 members E.R.A.S.A. is organised into eight regions, each of which consist of a number of clubs. A sophisticated computerised record system gives detailed information on every event which is organised. Endurance riding is popular as a family sport, as often several members take part together. That pure-bred and part-bred Arabians are by far the most popular mounts is borne out by an analysis of the horses in the 1994 Rand Endurance Club's annual endurance ride, one of the pre-qualifying rides for entry into the National Championships: 90 per cent of the top ten were of Arabian breeding.

Argentina

The A.A.C.C.A. (Asociacion Argentina de Criadores de Cababallos Arabes) was responsible for the first organised endurance ride in 1985. The President at that time was Mrs Claudia C. de Quentin and it was largely through her efforts that the ride took place on her farm in the South-East Section of the Province of Buenos Aires.

Riders were classified into three grades, light, medium and heavyweight, and with strict supervision under three vets the ride took place in glorious summer weather. The course took riders through woodland and along a section of the firm sandy beach of the Atlantic coast. The point of the ride was for competitors to complete the course within a given time and present a fit horse at the end. The following day a gymkhana was held with barrel and bending races.

There is now an annual long distance ride, combined with a show and held at a small sea-side resort on the Atlantic coast. The whole event is held over four days, the first two devoted to riding the 60 km course at an average of 15 km per hour, and under the supervision of three vets, mostly over loose sand and uneven ground, with some hard dirt roads.

The show takes place on the last two days. With the bonus of characteristic Argentinian hospitality and friendly and helpful attitudes on the part of everyone it is an occasion much enjoyed by all, the big barbecue in the evening being a highlight of the proceedings.

CHAPTER SIX

The versatile Arabian

Polo

Although the Arabian's forte is undoubtedly endurance, it can claim to be capable of competing with considerable success in most equine sport disciplines. Its use centuries ago for chariot racing, together with the game of stick and ball, has already been mentioned.

The Persian poet Firdausi wrote in his *Shah Nahmah* of a great match between Persians and Turks in 600 B.C. to celebrate peace between them, with the rival kings watching seated on a golden couch. The *Shah Nahmah* shows beautifully coloured and vivid illustrations of polo. The game is also mentioned in *The Rubaiyat of Omar Khayyam*: 'The ball no question makes of Ayes and Noes, But right or left as strikes the Player goes.' It spread east to China and is even said to have flourished in Japan about 700 B.C.

The Mogul emperors brought the game, then known as *chaugham*, to India; Akbar considered it the finest training for his officers. Manipur is said to have been the birthplace of the modern game of polo. Around 1850 the Manipurs introduced the game to the tea-growing district of Cachar where local officials and tea-planters became involved and largely through the efforts of Joe Sherar (who earned himself the sobriquet of 'The Father of Modern Polo') the Silchar Polo Club was formed in 1859. British cavalry officers posted at Cachar took up the game, and a polo of sorts was played at Dacca and Calcutta.

In 1983 Joe Sherar founded the Calcutta Polo Club and the following year he brought a team 'with beautiful little Manipuri ponies' to play there. The Indian blood-horses were of Arabian, Tataric and Turcoman descent, with many fresh infusions of Eastern blood from the vast trade in horses from the Arabian Gulf into India.

At that time there were seven players a side and the mallet resembled a hockey stick. The game soon spread like wild-fire. On returning to England in the early 1870s the 10th Hussars arranged a match with the 9th Lancers to be played at Hounslow Heath. The match was announced as 'Hockey on Horseback' and it was said that the ball used was a white ivory billiard ball! This match sparked off polo in England and several clubs were soon formed, including the famous Hurlingham Polo Club which was founded in 1874.

The ponies then used were only 13.3 hands but the height limit was gradually raised and by 1895 was 14.2 hands. Arabians and their crosses with small breeds were mostly used, but as the height limit rose small Thoroughbreds were brought in and gradually a different type of 'Polo Pony' emerged.

Pure-bred Arabians still take part in polo, however, and this was recently demonstrated by Rabando (Rabaat ex Velvet Haze), a 15.1 hh gelding. Rabando was bought in 1989 as a five year old by Jacqui Grossard and her brothers, John and Duncan. They had been seeking an all-round performer as Jacqui wanted a horse for dressage and her brothers wanted to play polo. The following year Rabando started playing at Cowdray, generally in two chukkas, and was soon classed as a fast low-medium goal pony. In 1990 Duncan, a member of the London University team, rode him in two-chukka tournaments at Ham and Cambridge; they were in the final of the Farewell Cup and scored the winning goal.

Meanwhile Jacqui had brought him on from dressage to one day events and hunter trials, and he proved to be a brilliant jumper.

In a fine demonstration of versatility, in 1991 during one summer week Rabando played three chukkas of polo, won a local open cross country and show-jumping, and was fifth in the Ridden Arab class at the South of England show. In polo he was in the final of the Park House Cup tournament and the semi-finals of the Farewell Cup.

Pig-sticking

The 'Gulf' Arabs, as those horses imported from the Arabian Gulf into India were sometimes called, were expected by their masters to do anything demanded of them. In between carrying an official or acting as a charger for an Army officer, they would race, play polo, take part in gymkhanas and go hunting or pig-sticking.

The writer S. A. H. A. A. Imam is in no doubt as to the ideal mount for pig-sticking. In *The Centaur* he gives a description of the type of horse required, in which the criteria are: unlimited quality; good natural balance to enable them to negotiate at speed blind trappy country, ridden on a loose rein; capacity to gallop at racing speed at least four to five miles; the bravery to take any jump and the gameness to carry on to the bitter end. Legs must stand iron-hard going, and lastly this paragon of animals must have the courage to face a charging boar. Imam then sums up by saying that all these attributes are best found in a well-bred animal of under 15.2 hands and that the Arabian is eminently suitable.

In support of these demands he quotes from Major Henry Shakespeare's *The Wild Sports of India* in which is written: 'Action is power – it is all in all; a horse without it, may do to look at – while standing still he may appear a magnificent animal, but he is not worth a shilling . . . Never buy anything but a high-caste horse as a hunter [pig-sticker].' He goes on to give an account of an experience he had at Hingolee in 1850 with his 'high blood bay Aneezah Arab' with which he claimed to have scarcely ever lost first spear. The horse was wounded by a boar and laid up for three weeks and had only been walked prior to his next hunt. They put up a nilgai, or 'blue bull' antelope, which had a quarter-mile start, but of the four well-mounted riders after two and a half miles only Major Shakespeare on his bay was up with the blue bull when the animal threw himself into a quicksand river and escaped. He wrote: 'Any but a pure-bred blood-horse would have been shut up in the first half mile, at the pace we went, if he had been subjected to such a trial; it is only the noble son of the desert that proves his noble descent on such occasions.'

Mention is made by Lt Colonel Fife, writing in his *Mosaic of Memories*, of a flea-bitten grey Arabian which was not only a perfect pig-sticker but which would in high grass follow the quarry by scent. Other references are made to the hunting of hyenas and leopards. Fife continues: 'When one considers the rather "woodeny" hunters, point-to-pointers and hacks which are the norm, riding a perfect pig-sticker in one of these capacities would surely be a revelation, always accepting that its comparatively small size may handicap it as a heavy-weight and for racing over big fences.' The reference to 'woodeny' is interesting, as Lady Anne Blunt writes in her Journals of a visitor to her stud who found other horses 'woodeny' when compared to the Blunts' Arabians – an expression which she found most apt concerning the difference.

Competitive Driving

Competitive Driving is another sport in which Arabians take part. In Carriage Driving, as described in the U.S.A., the horse has to pull a heavy carriage over different types of terrain, and execute various manoeuvres. The rules for F.E.I. Combined Driving (usually with a pair) were taken from eventing and adapted for driving, but with an additional section as the competition includes presentation when the whole turnout of horses, driver, vehicle and harness, is judged for cleanliness and soundness. Dressage on the first day is followed on the second day by a marathon with various hazards, tricky gates and obstacles set up over the course, which is divided into five sections of alternating trot and walk. The third day holds the obstacle course competition in which the driver has to navigate around cones and between gates without knocking off the balls set on top of the obstacles. The vet checks start before the event and continue periodically throughout the three days.

The first Combined Driving competition in the U.S.A., to include a full true cross-country course, was held at Millbrook, New York, on 4 and 5 May 1974. The natural obstacles included crossing a pond 30 feet wide and 2½ feet deep, up and down steep hills and along wooded trails. The only Arabian to compete, and the only stallion, was Muffet Ibn Safir (Al-Marah Safir ex Muffet Bin Yatez). He was placed third overall in the Single Horse Competition, winning the obstacle driving and placing well in the other two divisions, dressage and cross country.

A team of Arabians competing in advanced level dressage at Fair Hill, Maryland, U.S.A.

The pure-bred stallion Garlius (AM Canadius ex AM Lady Garland) competed very successfully in Carriage Driving, winning several championships and best condition awards in open competition. Foaled in 1973, he is a multi halter and show performance champion, including a Canadian Top Ten, Regional Championships and Top Fives, as well as American Horse Show Association English Pleasure Horse of the Year. His owners, having become disenchanted with the Arabian show world, decided to find a new way to enjoy their horses in competition and to compare them with other breeds, and so began to drive them. They attended a clinic run by an ex-Royal coachman, who had been used to driving horses of 16 to 18 hands – Garlius was at first referred to as a 'pony'. However, by the end of the clinic he had so impressed the instructor that he wanted to put Garlius in the lead of a four-in-hand of Warmbloods and go to a show the following week! Garlius was 13 when he began his career in driving and by competing and winning marathons and working classes he helped to dispel the initial prejudice against Arabians in this field, and by his perfect behaviour won over many who had been biased against the breed. His pure-bred daughter, Lake Hill Rhine Ice, has also won many championships in Combined Driving. Many people in the U.S.A. are now

Rhine Ice, winner of many combined driving championships, jumping into the water hazard. (Note the back wheels and driver's efforts to stay in the carriage.)

driving single or teams of Arabians and part-breds and in 1992 at a Carriage Association of America's annual meet Arabians were the best teams in the four-in-hand division. Another competitor chose Arabians because she had found them a pleasure to work with, and she commented that they 'are people orientated'.

Although a great number of pure-breds are driven in show classes in the U.S.A. many others are used just for pleasure, in countries all over the world. Some of the old European studs have for centuries driven pure-breds, or horses of the 'Arabian breed' (i.e. part-breds with as much as 95 per cent pure Arabian blood and thus of the type, conformation and soundness of the pure-bred). At one of the oldest, Babolna, south-west of Budapest, magnificent teams of five-in-hand impress visitors to the stud. One visitor to Babolna, writing in 1935, described finding under the shade of the great acacia the complete military band mounted on 28 grey Arab mares. The bandsmen, in striking national dress and playing national airs, ended with the famous Rakoczy March – best known, he adds, to Western Europe through Berlioz's *Faust*.

Al-Marah Garcon, successful in show driving classes in the U.S.A.

In the U.K. one of the first pure-breds to compete in three-day driving events was the gelding Blue Warrior (Barbe Bleu ex Stopa). In 1982, his first year, he was placed second or third in each of the six competitions entered and qualified for the National Championships. The following year in Open Horse events he was never out of the top five in strong competition, mostly against cobs and hackney crosses. In between driving events Blue Warrior was hunted and used for rounding up cattle. He was also ridden side-saddle and his owner's four-year-old son was taught to ride on him.

TOP *Five-in-hand at Babolna, Hungary.*

BELOW *Four-in-hand at A.H.S. Haydock, pure-bred Arabians.*

Team chasing

In 1995 four Arabians made history when they became the first team of pure-breds to take part in team chasing in the U.K. In this comparatively new sport at least three horses in each team of four must complete the course; the time of the third horse to finish is taken as the time for the team. Bogey Time is established by one of the organising committee riding the course the day before the event at a fair hunting pace. Competitors are not told the Bogey Time until results are announced at the end of the day, and stop watches are forbidden. The winning team is that which completes the course nearest to the Bogey Time.

The first appearance of the team, under the name 'The Arabian Knights', was at the Whaddon Chase Hunt Team Chase and Hunter Trials in October 1995. It consisted of two stallions, Shalkar (Mehneer ex Sherasa), who also has many successes in-hand including third at the 1995 National Show, and Samad (Diamond Star ex Shriphala), winner of Regional Group Versatile Horse competitions, and two geldings, Soberino (Procyon ex Shabana), who has twice been the A.H.S. Performance Horse of the Year and had success in long distance riding, and Roundhills Desert Novello (Linknumstar Isaac ex Silver Countess), another versatile performer and winner in one-day events. They were one of 50 teams entered in the Novice Team Chase in which 18 fences had to be jumped over a course of one and a quarter miles. It was judged on a Bogey Time of four minutes and thirty-one seconds and although they completed in four seconds less, six other teams were nearer the time target. However, competing in the Individual Hunter Trial over the same course but judged on the fastest horse through the 'timed section' to have a clear round, Linda Hannaford won on Soberino in a class of 92 entries.

The pure-bred mare Magic Miss (Grand Duke ex Kristil), who has competed with success in jumping and showing classes, substituted for Roundhills Desert Novello at the West Oxfordshire Riding Club event a week later. 'The Arabian Knights' came second, beaten by four seconds, in the Open Fun Team Chase, which was judged on the fastest time over the whole course. Samad and Soberino, singly and as a pair, also had first places in Hunter Trials that year.

Show classes

Classes for ridden Arabians have always featured in the Arab Horse Society shows, as well as some major shows in the U.K. Before the Second World War when there were not many studs and the Arabian population was comparatively small, most stallions were ridden and those which were shown in-hand often appeared on the same day under saddle – something which is rare today.

An outstanding example from those days of an Arabian competing successfully in both categories was Sainfoin (Rasim ex Safarjal) who won the stallion championship at the A.H.S. London show a record seven times between 1927 and 1936 and completed a 'double' by winning the ridden class as well in 1931, 1932 and 1936; in addition Sainfoin won a mile and a half race in 1929.

The last stallion to pull off a similar double was Argos (Nabor ex Arfa) who at the 1965 A.H.S. show won the senior stallion class and was reserve champion male and also the best ridden stallion.

Narim, by Moment ex Nejnaia, whose racing record in Russia was three wins and five seconds. A show winner in the U.K. and sire of champion stock, he won the Sire Produce Class at the 1989 A.H.S. Show.

Many people regret the modern division which can now dictate that there are 'show' stallions, exhibited only in-hand, or 'performance' ones. This has partly arisen through the current fashion for Arabians in general – and stallions in particular – to be shown in an unnecessarily flamboyant manner. A top-class Arabian stallion has natural 'presence' and style; there should be no need to create artificial exuberance simply to impress judges and spectators. Because of this present-day manner of showing, even though it is less pronounced in the U.K. than on the Continent and in America and some other countries, few stallions are shown both in-hand and under saddle. The somewhat hyped-up training some horses are given for showing in-hand obviously differs from that needed to ensure a well-schooled ride, and owners of ridden stallions can feel their horses are at a disadvantage when shown in-hand.

In the opinion of many any idea of there being a separation of in-hand show winners from those which are ridden is potentially harmful to the breed. Arabians always have been, and should continue to be, horses to ride. The ideal must be a horse which can compete successfully in-hand and also be capable of doing well under saddle. In 1995 the Arab Horse Society started a new competition which it is hoped will encourage owners to show their stallions in-hand and ridden at the same show. An innovation planned for 1996 is a Ridden Championship Show.

There have, of course, been some other stallions which have competed in both sections at the same show, or in the same year. Jazmir (Marania Gold ex Jazirah Sbeyel) was an international winner in-hand in 1983 and later was shown under saddle. He was champion both in-hand and ridden at a Regional Group show in 1986, and also won the novice ridden championship at the A.H.S. Northern show at Haydock and was the best novice under saddle at the A.H.S. show, Ascot, that year. Crystal Magician (Crystal King ex Sheer Magic) won numerous championships in-hand and then came out under saddle at the age of 11. The following year he was reserve ridden champion at Haydock and in 1993 overall champion in-hand and ridden champion on the same day at a Regional Group show; in 1994 he won the veteran class and was reserve national champion stallion.

Bright Cavalier (Bright Crown ex Soumana of Fairfield) had a notable success at the U.K. international show at Towerlands in 1990. He won the ridden stallion class with the highest points of the show to take the ridden championship, and also competed in-hand to come fifth in his class, which was won by the eventual reserve champion stallion. This achievement must be almost unique at an international show in Europe.

Amongst others over the last decade or so to have been successfully shown in-hand and under saddle are Vain Hussar (Argos ex Mirella), who

won many championships and in 1987 was overall male champion in-hand at Haydock and the best ridden stallion at the A.H.S. Ascot. He was later exported to the U.A.E.

Golden Flambeau (Silver Flame ex Masque) was second best colt in the international classes held at Ascot in 1978 and then went on to be shown under saddle. He was a consistent winner, including ridden champion at an international show in Switzerland and reserve champion pure-bred at A.H.S., Ascot, in 1987; he also became an accomplished dressage horse. Kazmierek (Barif ex Kazra El Saghira), who won at an international show in Europe as a yearling, was the ridden champion at Malvern in 1993. Rusleem (El Saleem ex Rullante) was senior male champion at international Towerlands in 1993, and the high point winner in-hand; and the same year was champion ridden novice at Haydock. Hadeir (Ralvon Elijah ex Nimet), foaled in 1986, was three times reserve British National Champion from 1988 to 1990, and when he came out under saddle took the pure-bred ridden championship at Haydock and was best ridden stallion at Malvern in 1993.

Bright Cavalier winning the Ridden Championship at Towerlands International Show in 1990; he also came fifth in-hand.

Kazmierek, in the Costume Class at Haydock. He was Supreme Ridden Champion at Malvern in 1993.

Rusleem, by El Saleem out of Rullante, in his first year under saddle in 1993 at Malvern. That year he was Novice Ridden Champion at Haydock and Senior Male Champion in-hand and Best British-bred High Points Male at Towerlands International.

It is hoped that in future many more exhibitors will accept the challenge and show their stallions in both sections. It can do nothing but good for the breed, and can but enhance sire demand if a stallion is exposed under saddle as well as in-hand in the same year.

In the U.K. judges generally ride all the horses in the ordinary ridden classes, which is rarely done in most other countries. Horses are shown at the walk, trot, canter and gallop, after which they are called into line in initial order and the judge rides. Saddles are then removed and the horse appraised for conformation and type, and trotted out for the judge to study its action. With riders remounted they are then placed in the final order. Judging this way is quite a lengthy process but it does ensure that the horse's manners and paces are as thoroughly assessed as its performance and general appearance with its own rider.

The size and standard of ridden Arabian classes in the U.K. has risen steadily over the last two decades. An increasing number of mares are now appearing under saddle, and at many Regional Group shows there are separate classes for them. This is to be commended as it is important that potential brood mares should prove their ability, as well as the stallions. Some very high quality geldings are now appearing, both in-hand and under saddle. They do as well as entires in open competition against other breeds, and are equally effective as ambassadors for the Arabian.

At the A.H.S. National Show in 1994 there were two ridden classes for pure-bred stallions, two for mares and three for geldings; in addition Anglo-Arabs had one and part-breds three classes, the latter divided by height. Junior riders are catered for and there is an open pairs class and side-saddle. The championship for supreme ridden exhibit has reached a very high standard indeed.

Taking the winners over the eleven years from 1985, only one Anglo-Arab has succeeded in taking the title, Mountwood Aviation (Desert Faro ex Alf's Folly), who won in 1992. Far from being eclipsed by the stallions, pure-bred mares have more than held their own. The winner in 1985 was Bright Dancer (Rayyan ex Bright Dawn). Liquidambar (Indian Diadem ex Bright Reflexion) won in 1989 and 1991, and Chalyska (General Gold ex Chantilla) in 1994, whilst the gelding Clearly Great (Fari II ex Clarity) much to his credit won successively in 1987 and 1988. The three stallion winners were Silver Satyr (Silver Chastindi ex Shamasque) in 1986, Al Maurab (Ben Rabba ex Al Malika) in 1990 and Kazmierek's 1993 win. Another mare, Caramanda (Crystal Magician ex Maracanda), won in 1995.

The gelding Agar Apparant (Royal Blue ex Pendle Atlanta) is one of many part-breds who have carried the torch for horses of Arabian breeding in open competition. As a yearling he was unbeaten in eight outings and

ABOVE *Winners of the Pairs Class at Malvern, 1991, Xafir (Blue Grotto ex Xarifa) and White Cascade (White Lightning ex Velvet Shadow).*

Carrik Crystif (Crystal King ex Nazif) competing in the side-saddle class at A.H.S. Ascot, 1986.

since starting his career under saddle he has gained an impressive record in open hack classes. Brought out at the age of four, a good season in 1988 culminated in a fourth at the Royal International Show. The following year in 11 outings he was never placed lower than second, including reserve champion at the National Hack and Cob Show. A brilliant season was crowned by winning the Hack of the Year award at the Horse of the Year Show at Wembley.

Many Riding Club members own horses of Arabian breeding, and one club, East Grinstead, attracted much acclaim when their team won at the twenty-first Quadrille of the Year in 1987. Initially a team of three – Partridge Simon, by the pure-bred Gerwazy out of an unregistered mare; Ronley Theodore by the part-bred Astley Amber Affair; and the Anglo, Bonny Lass by Benara – the Club won at Windsor, South of England and the Royal International. Then, joined by the part-bred Fleetmead Fiesta (an accomplished dressage performer by Carbrooke Surprise out of Cornish Fanfare), the team was one of four to qualify for the finals at the Horse of the Year Show. Judges Richard Meade and Jane Kidd commented: 'good

British National Supreme Ridden Champion 1989 and 1991, Liquidambar at the A.H.S. Show, Kempton Park, 1989.

Riding Club's Teams of Three Championship at the Royal International Show. Three part-bred sisters, Fleetmead Finesse, Fleetmead Facade and Fleetmead Fiesta, from East Grinstead Riding Club.

mixture of drama and effective technical content. It was entertaining and ended all too soon.'

Ridden classes are not as popular on the Continent as they are in the U.K. and such countries as Australia, New Zealand and South Africa, where they are an important part of the show scene. The U.S.A. and Canada probably have the widest range of events from show hack, hunter pleasure, to trail, stock-horse, working cow-horse, and many others. However, there is considerable controversy about some of the American classes. Park Horse, for example, has become very exaggerated and the high and somewhat jerky knee action now fashionable is such a parody of the true Arabian way of

going it means that severe training by artificial means has to be adopted to alter the horse's natural movement. English Pleasure is stilted with the knee action again too high to be natural, and Western Pleasure has also become distorted, with the horses made to carry their heads unnaturally low. The Western Working classes, however, are different, with no dependence on show-ring fashion or gimmickry. It is sad to see the Arabian's beautifully free and gay movement deliberately falsified to suit the style demanded of some showing classes.

Winning Quadrille at the 1985 Horse of the Year Show. The East Grinstead team of part-breds, Partridge Simon, Rouley Theodore, Fleetmead Facade and Fleetmead Fiesta.

Western riding

Enthusiasm for Western riding has spread from America to many countries around the world. Although these events are largely aimed at Quarter Horses, a growing number of Arabians now take part with considerable success.

147

The U.S.A. and Canada have a variety of Western classes at their all-Arabian shows, and at National Arabian shows in South Africa and Australia Western Pleasure is included. In Europe, Germany and Sweden host a number of Western events but apart from Reining, at which Arabians are particularly adept, most are directed at Quarter Horses.

The Western Horseman's Association of Great Britain was formed in 1968. Its main aim is to set and constantly maintain a high standard of horsemanship and turnout. It has a steadily growing membership and with qualified instructors and judges it has instituted a series of recognised examinations in Western horsemanship.

There are now establishments which specialise in producing horses for all types of Western work and also run demonstrations and training clinics. In addition to instruction in horsemanship, the aspect of fun wherever there is involvement with horses and riding is not forgotten.

Classes for Western riding are held at a number of shows in the U.K. and the W.H.A. runs a Championship Show each year with a great variety of classes included in the two-day schedule. These range from Western Pleasure, Showmanship, Horsemanship, Working Cow Horse, Stock Horse and Cattle Cutting to Pole Bending, Barrel and other races, and Trail and Versatility. Championships are awarded on a high-point system in three sections, Cattle, Pleasure and Games.

An Arabian mare with an exceptional record is Shazara (Shadrac ex Sierra Sky) who has been a performance champion since 1986 and in 1995 she retained her status as Cattle Champion. Another mare competing successfully in Western classes is Dahookah, a daughter of Dahshan and Gai Warsaw, a stallion who came on lease to the U.K. from the U.S.A. where he had been Champion Western Stock Horse and won top honours at many shows. Other pure-breds are used in demonstrations of Western Riding around Britain.

National Western Champion, Shazara, by Shadrac out of Sierra Sky.

CHAPTER SEVEN

Olympic disciplines

Jumping

Some of the fallacious comments made about Arabians are to the effect that they cannot jump, will not go through water, or are 'fizzy'! It can only be assumed that these assertions are made by those who have no personal experience of working with the breed.

There are numerous instances on record of Arabians showing great prowess and bold jumping ability in the hunting field. Before the advent of the motor car, Arabians took their place with other breeds and were used for general riding, driving, and for hunting. The jumping ability of the early imported stallions Maidan and Kars has already been mentioned; Kars was not the only Arabian Wilfrid Blunt hunted. In the early days of the Crabbet stud all the stallions and most of the mares were ridden and driven in harness.

Miss Etheldred Dillon, who had a stud of Arabian horses in the latter part of the nineteenth century, owned the mare Raschida (Kars ex Wild Thyme), who is said to have won 19 first prizes in jumping competitions and carried 13 stone to hounds. Her finest achievement was at the age of 15 when, having been entered with a foal at foot in the brood mare class, she competed in the High Wall Jumping Competition in Dublin in 1898. Against 20 renowned Irish hunters she came second and a quoted press report said: 'The old mare cleared the fences neatly at a canter and only lost first place by knocking off a small pebble.'

Mr D.E. Neale, whose stud was started in 1925, bought the mare Rish (Nejran ex Rabla) and her son Rishan (by Nadir) and writing about his stud said of Rish: 'She was too old to breed again, but was still able to a do a day's hunting at the age of 25.'

Lady Yule, owner of the famous Hanstead Stud, bred Halil Sherif (Nuri Sherif ex Razina) who was hunted with the Heythrop Hunt. He was

Naplyv, by Pomeranets out of Nitochka, jumping into the water splash at the A.H.S. Raynham one-day event.

described as a wonderful hunter, and jumped anything he was asked in perfect style. Later he was trained for dressage and gave a display at the International Horse Show, Olympia, in 1934.

It has sometimes been asserted that the Arabian's size is detrimental to their capacity to make good hunters, but what they lack in height is amply made up for by their courage and strength, and written evidence frequently records that weights of 13 stone or more were carried with ease. Today pure-bred, Anglo-Arab and part-bred Arabians are regularly appearing in the hunting field, and are also often seen competing in show-jumping and eventing.

An international show-jumper of renown was Rex the Robber, by the pure-bred Noran out of the Thoroughbred Berenice. Ridden by Alwin

Schockemöhle, he won many of the most important trophies in the 1970s including the Puissance in Amsterdam and Dublin.

In 1972 a pure-bred stallion bred in England was making a name for himself as a show-jumper in Sweden. Caranto (Manto ex Comfort's Caravel), then six years old, was competing in open classes with anything from 50 to 100 entrants. He had five wins and four seconds and in one competition he beat 107 horses.

An Arabian to have represented Britain in show-jumping is the gelding Silent King (Dancing King ex Silent Dove), who reached Grade J.A. in 1980, after winning numerous championships at novice and intermediate level. That year Silent King was picked for the Junior International event at Copenhagen. Six nations took part, and in five competitions he won two, came second twice, and was third in the fifth. In 13 rounds, he had only one fence down – in the jump-off of the class in which he came third. In addition to his brilliant career as a show-jumper, Silent King won a race at Hawthorn Hill, and he also won the first Ride and Tie in England.

Many other Arabians have competed successfully in show-jumping. Those who have qualified for Junior Events include the stallion Bojan (Haroun ex Star Flight) who was trained and ridden by a 17 year old. During the 1980s he qualified several times for junior Foxhunter and was also consistently highly placed in junior Newcomers. El Kaasha (Kaaba ex Shamana), a 15 hh gelding, was another who made a name for himself. By 1989 he had won £270 at affiliated show-jumping and qualified for the Area

The Shagya stallion, Grande Arabe, by Galan II out of Ayusha, show-jumping.

Foxhunter finals, with four double clear rounds. In one competition El Kaasha jumped a five foot Puissance wall and consequently won the class.

In the U.S.A. the stallion Debs Dancing Prince (Azrhand ex Heyoka) set a record when clearing six foot in the High Jump at Colorado State Fair in 1981. The following year he won Open Jumper Class and Championship and also the High Jump.

One of the greatest Arabian horses in American show-jumping, however, was the gelding Senrab (Potif ex Mufissa), foaled in 1953. He was only 14.3 hh but during the 1960s he became famous for his talented jumping. He was shown only in open classes and won numerous competitions. One of his most remarkable wins was the Open Junior stakes at Pomona during his first year together with the 'Green' (Novice) Jumper class – winning both was very unusual. Senrab jumped walls as high as six foot four inches and consistently cleared six-foot-high jumps, as well as spread fences six foot wide and five foot in height. He was a great character and is said to have been at his best performing before 'packed houses'; the wilder the applause the better he jumped! He would leap any kind of obstacle he was put to, from stacked-up wheelbarrows to tractors. He continued competing until nearing 20, and even after his retirement did some exhibition jumping and was a tuition mount for pupils under instruction at the Parnell Girls' School in California, where he spent most of his life.

In 1982 an Egyptian-bred Arabian gelding, Feydan, was ranked amongst the top 15 international show-jumpers in the F.E.I. World Competition held in Kuwait. With his young rider, Naddia Al Mutawa, he had two clear rounds and won the Jawad Bu Khamseen Trophy against 22 rivals. After two more important wins they were awarded the F.E.I. Certificate for the top show-jumper in Kuwait, and Feydan's consistency earned him a place in the Kuwait team for the Asian games held in India that year. In the jump-off for the Championship Feydan was the only horse to have three clear rounds and the last was also the fastest time so he deservedly won the Gold Medal.

With so many horses of Arabian breeding competing in show-jumping in the U.K. in the 1990s, classes are now held at the A.H.S. National Show at Malvern. Some of the Regional Group shows also hold jumping classes as encouragement to members – some enter for the fun of it and some with the more serious object of going on into open competition or to the classes at Malvern. The courses are graded from those for novices up to jumps of three foot six inches and include Anglo-Arabs and part-breds. An enthusiastic welcome to the introduction of jumping at Malvern in 1991 was presented by Betty Finke, a writer from Germany; reporting on the A.H.S. show she said: 'a large number of pure-breds tackled it with enthusiasm and ability'.

Stallions, mares and geldings can all compete, and in 1994 there were nine classes from Novice to Open, with championship classes divided between pure-breds, Anglo-Arabs and part-breds, as well as a Regional Groups team competition.

Linda Hannaford and Samad, by Diamond Star out of Shriphala, second in the pure-bred jumping class at Malvern in 1993.

Eventing

Many Arabians who compete in show-jumping also take part in eventing, which of course includes dressage. Sky Scimitar (Dancing King ex Sable Sky) won the Junior Ridden Gelding class at the A.H.S. show in 1978 before going on to compete successfully in unaffiliated dressage. At the same time he was performing creditably in show-jumping and cross-country events. In 1983 with wins in the Team One-Day Event at Russell Farm, and at Park Farm in both team and individual dressage, and a second in the Team Prix Caprilli, he qualified for the National Finals.

A pure-bred stallion who appeared in B.H.S. horse trials in the 1980s was the 15 hh General Lee Gold (General Gold ex Leda), whose rider's identity soon declared itself as 'the chap who rides the Arab'! In addition to success in the show-ring, both in-hand and under saddle, he was the first pure-bred to compete successfully, at Senior Affiliated level, in all three main disciplines – eventing, show-jumping and dressage. He gained 38 B.H.S. points in very few outings, qualifying for both the Novice and the Novice-Elite Championships. He also won hunter trials, and qualified for the British Airways National Championship on his first outing. Throughout his five year career in eventing, hunter trials and drag-hunting he carried 13 stone.

Arabians competing in three-day events are not from one country only. In 1962 the 14.3 hh stallion Ferishal (Ferhal ex Rishafieh), bred in the U.S.A. but owned by Mrs Trethewey of Canada, took part in the famous Three-Day Event at Pebble Beach in California. A full hand smaller than the other horses in his team, Ferishal gave a brilliant performance over the cross-country course of 11 miles and 29 jumps, and with a good round in the show-jumping helped his team win the Bronze Medal. A Californian writer in *The Arabian Horse World* said: 'An Arab named Ferishal came down from Canada to do a tremendous job for the breed! I cannot tell you what an impression this little horse made on the spectators! People I know as detractors of the Arab were all exclaiming over him!'

If further proof of the Arabian's ability in eventing were needed it is provided by the 14.3 hh bay gelding Hal (Ebn El Hamra ex Opal) bred in Denmark and owned by the Lowe family. Hal was bought as a rather shy untrained three year old but after initial training by Marianne Lowe he became the mount of her 12-year-old son, Kim.

At first Kim rode Hal around the countryside with only a halter. They went up and down the side of a quarry, swam lakes and jumped a wide variety of obstacles, ranging from tables to fences, thoroughly enjoying it all. After two years they started to enter jumping competitions and won nearly every time, for Hal never made mistakes and also proved to be fast.

By this time Hal had grown over the limit for pony competition but it was decided to try taking on the bigger horses and more success followed. Having shown that he was brave and careful across country, in 1988 at the age of six it was decided to start eventing and his dressage training began. This discipline was not quite so much to Hal's liking, but he adapted to the schooling and the following year he won the award of Working Arab of the Year. In 1990 when Kim was 16 and by far the youngest rider and Hal the smallest horse, they won the Danish Championship in Cross Country.

The big breakthrough came in 1991 when Kim and Hal started in Intermediate eventing and had four wins and a second in the National Competition. The next year they won the Nordic Young Rider Championship near Oslo and repeated their victory in 1993, when the Championships were held in Finland. In these two years Hal and Kim headed the Land Rover Top Ten in Denmark. In all, Hal won 42 first prizes,

OPPOSITE ABOVE *Kim Lowe and Hal at Knuthenborg, 1991.*

OPPOSITE BELOW *Kim Lowe and Hal at Lyon D'Angeres, 1993.*

11 seconds and 5 thirds, before Kim's increasing height forced him to retire from riding Hal.

These are only a few of the Arabians which in growing numbers are competing in eventing around the world. However, it can be appreciated that some riders prefer a larger horse and for them the Anglo-Arab or part-bred may be more suitable. Anglo-Arabs and part-breds have also had great success in show-jumping.

Two part-bred Arabs won the Badminton Horse Trials in the 1960s. Jonathon, by the pure-bred Amigo, won in 1967, following success at Tidworth and Chatsworth the previous year when he was the 1966 Points Champion. In 1969 Richard Walker rode Pasha, by the pure-bred Rudan, to victory at Badminton and was also second in the European Horse Trials, less than two points behind the winner. A third part-bred of International standard was Shaitan, by Count Orlando, who won the Burghley Trials in 1969 and was reserve for the Olympic Team in Mexico.

Pirate VII, by the pure-bred Gerwazy, was the winner of B.H.S. two-day events. He also played second fiddle in the film *International Velvet*, and during filming he was the only horse to carry his actor-owner over a full set of Olympic show jumps.

Scintella, by Scindian Magic, won the Bramham Park three-day event, whilst two three-quarter bred Arabians by Scindian Magic, Magic Moments and Halcyon Days, won innumerable one-day events and combined training, as well as jumping, working hunter and riding horse classes.

In the World Championship at Lexington, U.S.A., in 1978, a horse in the New Zealand team named Bandolier, who was by an Arabian and out of a Thoroughbred mare, caught the eye of Lucinda Prior-Palmer (as she was then). She persuaded her sponsors to buy him and his name was changed to Mairingi Bay. He and Lucinda began competing in cross-country events in the U.K. In 1981 they enjoyed successes abroad and at home including the Advanced at Dauntsey and at Chatsworth. The next year Lucinda's husband, David Green, took over the ride and Mairingi Bay continued with distinction, finally winning the prestigious Gatwick Park One-Day Event in 1983 when he was 13 years old.

Spinning Rhombus, ridden by Andrew Nicholson at the 1993 Burghley Horse Trials.

A top-class three-day event horse in recent years has been Spinning Rhombus, a part-bred by the Thoroughbred Magic Circle out of a mare by the Arabian Tammany. When six years old he was sent to Andrew Nicholson, a member of the New Zealand team who was training horses in Somerset. The first big win they had was the Punchestown Three-Day Event where Spinning Rhombus was one of only three rounds without jumping or time penalties over a very severe cross-country course which eliminated 31 of the 53 competitors.

The outstanding performance came in the 1990 World Equestrian Games held at Stockholm, where they were in the Gold Medal winning New Zealand team. Spinning Rhombus was one of only three competitors to go clear across country within the time limit. This put them in line for the Bronze but sadly fences down in the show-jumping dropped him to fourth place, but he was still the second-highest placed horse in the team.

The French have developed their Anglo-Arabs to a high standard and as performance horses they have a very good record. To name just one, L'Aiglonne was the only horse to have a plus score across country in the 1948 Olympic Games and he was awarded the Gold Cup for his performance.

Dressage

The art of high-school riding has been practised on the Continent of Europe for centuries, and dressage competitions took place there long before this advanced expression of horsemanship became an established discipline in the U.K. Displays of *haute école* by the Lipizzaners of the famous Spanish Riding School, which are held in the impressive riding hall built in 1729–35 as part of the Hofburg in Vienna, are well known. Like many Continental breeds, Lipizzaners carry an element of Arabian blood. The original horses brought to Lipica, the founding stud of the Lipizzaner, came from Spain and their descendants have been recorded as a breed since 1735. Today all Lipizzaners trace to six stallions, one of which was the Arabian Siglavy (foaled in 1810), and nineteen mares, five of them Arabians.

Marion Winkler and Garbon, competing in dressage in Germany.

Colonel Hannes Handler, Director of the Spanish Riding School from 1965 to 1974, rode Arabian horses whilst on holiday one year – he was curious to see how they could perform in dressage. He trained one stallion in particular, named Rashad Ibn Nazeer, every day and was astonished at how quickly he learnt and how elegantly and willingly he performed. On a later visit Colonel Handler was amazed to find how much Rashad had remembered what he had been taught and how much he enjoyed performing.

The introduction of dressage into the U.K. was very largely due to the outstanding talent and enthusiasm of Henry Wynmalen, born Wijmalen in the Netherlands in 1889, who settled in Britain in 1927. Wynmalen became an authority and published the key work *Dressage: A Study of the Finer Points of Riding* in 1953. In 1961 he was honoured by the British Horse Society for his outstanding contribution and presented with their Gold Medal; his other books have already been mentioned in an earlier chapter.

Mr Wynmalen bought a grey Shagya stallion known as Basa (registered Shagya-XII-3) who was bred in Hungary and brought to England by an Army officer who had to sell him when posted overseas. The Shagya breed was founded at Babolna in Hungary, and descends from an Arabian stallion of that name who was imported from Syria. Prince Pückler-Muskau, whilst on travel, particularly admired Shagya's perfect symmetry and powerful build when he saw him in 1839. His stock became much sought after and popular for their toughness and endurance. A group of Shagya's descendants from a few mares, not strictly pure-bred but carrying much Arabian blood, were separately recorded at Babolna and after interbreeding and careful selection developed into a very fine type with strong Arabian characteristics, eventually to be known as a distinct breed. Most Shagyas today are of over 90 per cent Arabian blood, and this was very apparent in the beautiful little grey Basa. Wynmalen gave superb dressage displays with Basa at the Royal Windsor Shows and on other occasions, and also used him for lectures and demonstrations. His wife, Julia, has spoken these words: 'it is fair to say that he has had an incalculable influence on the awareness and importance of dressage for the British rider'.

Dressage, of course, has to be performed as a section of eventing, but it has also become a popular discipline on its own in the U.K. The A.H.S. includes dressage at its National Show and also holds an inter-group competition.

A pure-bred Arabian who reached international standard in dressage was Golden Wings (Bright Shadow ex Silent Wings). In 1980 he represented the U.K. in Belgium and at the Goodwood International meeting where he was the highest placed British entry competing in Prix St George, and his

Henry Wynmalen and Basa.

rider won the saddle awarded to the British entrant gaining the most points through the three days of competitions.

Many Arabians in the U.K. are now trained for dressage and compete at various levels. A unique partnership seen at the 1991 National Show at Malvern was that of Debbie Gulliford and the pure-bred gelding, Moon Warrior (Magic Argosy ex Dancing Moondust), for Debbie rode with a paralysed right arm and damaged leg, the result of a motor accident six years earlier. She and Moon Warrior built up a wonderfully understanding partnership and began competing in 1989, winning their class at the Riding for the Disabled (R.D.A.) National Dressage Championships and then representing the R.D.A. at the Riding Club Championships. With more successes the following year, when again representing the R.D.A., including an individual first at the Riding Club Championship, they were selected to represent the U.K. at the 1991 R.D.A. World Dressage Championship held at Aarhus, Denmark, where they won three fifth places.

Anglo-Arabs and part-breds are also competing with success in high-level dressage. Undoubtedly the best known in recent years is the Anglo gelding Prince Consort who is by the Thoroughbred Regal Boy out of the Scindian Magic daughter, Scindian Enchantress, who had a brilliant show career and produced nine foals. She was twice Junior Female Champion Anglo-Arab at the National Show and the Female Champion for five successive years from 1971 to 1975, and won 35 championships at county shows. Shown under saddle she won many prizes in Hack and ridden Anglo-Arab and part-bred classes, including fourth in the Show Hack of the Year at Wembley.

Prince Consort was launched into an international career at the age of eight, shortly after his first Grand Prix competition when he went as reserve in the British team to the 1984 Olympic Games; he was also selected for the

Diana Mason with Prince Consort.

next Games. Ridden by Diana Mason he represented Britain in several competitions in the U.K. and on the continent, most notably in Zuidlaren, Holland, where he was seventh in the Grand Prix. In 1988 he won the Country Life Dressage to Music at the Royal International Show, beating such horses as Dutch Gold and Maple Zenith, and the following year he came second at the European Championships in Luxembourg in musical freestyle, and also won the National Championship when scoring top marks in the Grand Prix at Goodwood. A brilliant year ended with Prince Consort becoming the Dressage Horse of the Year at Wembley.

All around the world pure-breds, part-bred and Anglo-Arabs are demonstrating their ability in dressage, but space does not allow details of the large number of horses of Arabian breeding who now compete in open competition. To mention just one, the British-bred gelding Kitwell Consul (seven-eighths Arabian blood, being by Indian Blizzard out of Cumberland Gift of the Fairies) took part in F.E.I. level dressage after his exportation to the U.S.A., and in 1989 aged 15 was said to be the best horse of Arab breeding competing at this level at that time. He won many state and zone dressage competitions in the States and was Champion in Prix St George that year in the United States Dressage Federation against all breeds.

Although the larger type of horse is more popular with dressage riders (certainly this is the case in Europe) there are many who prefer to watch the lighter breeds performing; somehow they airily convey the impression of needing less effort from their riders. Anyone who was fortunate enough to have watched Henry Wynmalen and Basa will never forget the consummate artistry of their performances.

Henry Wynmalen riding Basa at the A.H.S. Summer Show at Roehampton.

CHAPTER EIGHT

Planning for the future

Performance testing

It has been shown in the previous chapter how over the last 20 years or so there has been cautious expansion of the Arabian's participation in the 'sporthorse' world of dressage, combined training, and jumping. Bias against the breed may still exist among some, but it is being slowly vanquished by the performances of those pure-breds, Anglos and part-breds which venture forth and are seen to do well in open competition.

Some countries are beginning to evaluate the records of horses of Arabian breeding in performance. Some have general stallion testing schemes in which horses of all breeds are encouraged to take part, and in a few it is obligatory for a stallion to pass the test before he is allowed a licence to stand at stud.

In the U.K. the Arab Horse Society runs a premium scheme. In an attempt to improve the image of the Arabian in relation to the equine world in general, the Society joined with other breed societies to performance test its stallions under the auspices of the National Stallion Association (NASTA). Stallions are tested in dressage, show-jumping and cross country; Arabians are also assessed for conformation by a panel of three A.H.S. judges; they are graded on their results as Elite, Grade A, or B, and premiums awarded accordingly. There is also a premium scheme for mares which meet the criteria in showing and performance.

In 1993, with 17 stallions from four breed societies entered in the Test, an Arabian was the High Points winner over all other stallions. Galerito, by Galero out of Oba, has competed in open competition, unaffiliated and affiliated dressage and show-jumping, one-day events and hunter trials, at which he has nearly always won or been placed. He enjoys show-jumping most, and he has been very successful in Newcomers and Foxhunter classes. In the Stallion Performance Test Galerito achieved an almost faultless

round in the cross country, and with very high marks for character, temperament and overall impression he passed as Grade 1 in the NASTA rating and Grade A for an A.H.S. premium. Three other Arabians were awarded Grade A A.H.S. premiums: Imman (Marawan ex Mantella), Imad (Golden Cavalier ex Ivory Wings) and Zorab (Haroun ex Zulika).

Twenty years ago in Germany performance testing was obligatory before any stallion could be issued with a licence. By 1994, however, this no longer applied to pure-bred breeding under the W.A.H.O. (World Arabian Horse Organisation) ruling; but pure-bred stallions to be used on mares of any other breeding have to be performance tested. The test is in three sections of (*a*) a 100-day training period in dressage, show-jumping and jumping, (*b*) racing and (*c*) endurance of 60 or 80 km at an average speed, according to the age of the horse.

In 1974, at the age of seven, the Arabian Neron was entered in the stallion performance trials at Medingen and won the highest marks. His evaluation was 'walk and trot good, gallop excellent. Disposition and character very good; hard constitution. Very good attitude at work. Cross

Arab Performance show at Hamburg, 1990. On left, R. T. Mutabar, with his grandsire, Marwan, who is a champion in-hand and three times winner of the 100 mile Hamburg to Hanover endurance ride.

country course very good, great jumping ability. Complete result very good. Special remarks: a hard, versatile horse. Best in the race gallop.' Neron became one of the most remarkable stallions in open competition in Germany and he was a genuine family horse.

ABOVE *Show and performance winners in Germany. From left, Mahrani, in-hand champion; Marwan, in-hand and endurance champion; Mardschan, successful in dressage and goes in harness; Winettka; R. T. Royd Naggaf, in-hand champion.*

Neron, the genuine family horse, with Betty Peitzen on a cross-country course.

Bred in Russia, by Sport out of Nitochka, he stood 15.3 hh. The Peitgens acquired him when he was five years old and he came to them with a reputation of having a difficult disposition. They soon discovered his problem and how to solve it: given plenty of exercise and allowed to run out with mares he soon proved to have the best of temperaments. Neron was hunted regularly by Mr Peitgen and eventually the elder daughter Sylvia, then aged nine, became Neron's regular rider. She started competing in open jumping competitions; he was soon winning and came to be widely admired as a show-jumper.

In 1975 Neron was champion stallion at the Salon du Cheval in Paris. He was an excellent hunter and won many cross-country and three-day events. He was also trained for dressage and appeared at numerous shows ridden by Sylvia or Betty, the younger daughter by two years. At the age of 15 and after ten years of hard work he had perfectly sound legs and was still winning competitions. With such a brilliant career he was much sought after as a sire and had sometimes as many as 50 mares in a season; many of his progeny became successful show-jumpers and competition horses.

On 27 July 1985, Canada held its first Challenge of the Breeds at the Annual Edmonton Klondike Days. As part of the Horse Extravaganza ten breed associations fielded one horse each to compete in six events: Trail Horse, Barrel Racing, Roadsters in Harness, Open Hunter, Western Pleasure and English Pleasure. After a slow start in the trail class the 11-year-old Arabian stallion Pietrak made a strong showing in the next five events to get the top score of 54 points and beat his nearest contender, the Quarter Horse, by 6 points, with the Pinto third with 45 points. Pietrak's training for the event had begun in April but it was not until he won the elimination round at the Arabian Selection process in June that it was known that he was chosen to represent his breed.

In the U.S.A. there are now many Arabians, as well as Anglo-Arabs and part-breds, competing against other breeds in open competition. One reason put forward by a spokeswoman of the I.A.H.A. for the upsurge of pure-breds competing in hunter/jumper events was that there is a trend 'towards the Arabian being used more for the owner, rather than just staying at the trainer's barn as an investment'. Prejudice by some judges who were used to seeing horses of Thoroughbred or hunter type in these classes is being overcome. A revealing remark was heard concerning the Arabian Sweet William, who was A.H.S.A. Zone 8 Champion Arabian Hunter/Jumper in 1988, to the effect that 'the people who rode Sweet William worked with Thoroughbreds. They just couldn't believe what good minds Arabians have . . . they are so tractable and trainable.'

In 1986 the Arabian Sport Horse Association (A.S.H.A.I.) was founded to foster the sporting potential of the Arabian, Anglo-Arab, part-bred and Shagya: it now has members across the U.S.A., and in other countries. Its goal is actively to encourage and promote the use of horses of Arabian breeding in specific disciplines – combined training, dressage, driving (combined and pleasure), endurance, hunter and jumper. The Senrab Cup, a special high point annual award for outstanding achievement, was first presented in 1990.

There is concern in the U.S.A. that at All-Arabian shows in certain classes, principally show hack, hunter pleasure and dressage, the manner in which the horses are shown and judged has grown away from the 'traditional' presentation still seen in these classes at open shows. This would appear to be following the same pattern as the showing in-hand of Arabians, where the 'modern' style of exhibiting them, 'stretched' and with the head held high so that the beautiful arch of throat cannot be seen at all, is vastly different from the 'traditional' way of posing. As has already been said, there are many who feel that there is a tendency in all these 'fashionable' methods of showing, both in-hand and in some ridden classes, to try to alter the carriage and even the looks of the Arabian merely to suit a current fad. A.S.H.A.I. believes that it is important for Arabians to compete in open competitions and to do this successfully they must be trained in traditional style, and not as some appear when at the U.S. Arabian National Championships.

In 1985 an organisation, S.I.B.A., was started in Sweden to encourage owners of Arabians to participate in several disciplines; a growing number of Arabians are now competing at top levels. At the Three-Day S.I.B.A. Summer Games in 1994 there were 300 entries in the various events: dressage, show-jumping, military (three-day events), racing, driving and western riding. The title of S.I.B.A. Champion went for the first time to a mare, Karanta (Karnawal ex Esperanta), who excelled in military, show-jumping and racing.

The Swiss Arab Horse Society collates performance records of horses of Arabian breeding in the following disciplines: dressage, jumping, combination of showing and dressage, combination of showing and western riding, endurance, combination of endurance and dressage, three-day eventing and driving. The most versatile is arrived at via a points system, and in 1993 the winner was the pure-bred Bafran El Shachad, by Bafran El Sharai (who is also a competition horse) out of Libura. Most of the competitions in which the marks are given are open to all breeds. An organisation in Germany, the 'Beduin' German Arabian Rider Association, has just started to collect records of all horses of Arabian breeding which achieve success in all the different ridden sports.

Driving for pleasure in Switzerland, Roshak by Shah Jehan out of Rosmalika.

Around the world Arabian mares and geldings have also given abundant proof of versatility. To give one example in the U.K., Splendour of Sind did just about everything with enormous flair, a splendid exemplar of the abundant spirits and *joie de vivre* of the Arabian character.

A bay gelding by Shifari out of Scindia foaled in 1966, he joined the Roberts family in Sussex at the age of four, and his long career began when he made his debut in the show-ring that year and was British National Champion Gelding. For three years running he won the Ridden Gelding cup and in 1975 pulled off a unique double, winning both the in-hand and ridden championship at the A.H.S. show. Splendour of Sind loved jumping; out hunting he was said to cause much mirth as after negotiating an obstacle he considered difficult he would give his 'comic turn', described by his owner as 'an Arabian dance of triumph'. Followers of the hunt expressed surprise that an Arabian could go so well across country – in those days there were not so many pure-breds appearing out hunting.

The next enterprise was to teach him to go in harness. Indignation at first at being restricted by the shafts was overcome with care and tact and two years later he appeared in public and won five cups in open driving competitions during 1977. Again his sense of fun rose to the surface when, knowing that after receiving a rosette under saddle it is customary to canter round the ring, he insisted on trying to do the same in harness – his undignified exit causing much amusement. Splendour of Sind had a long and varied career as a performance horse. He won over 600 prizes in working hunter, riding horse and ridden Arabian classes and in horse trials, hunter trials, dressage, combined training, side-saddle and gymkhana, as well as private driving and driving marathon. For four years running he won the A.H.S. Dinsdale Trophy for the most versatile Arabian and with it all he gave the Roberts family immense pleasure and enjoyment.

Obviously the manner in which young Arabians are brought up will affect their later behaviour to a certain extent, but it is in their nature to be companionable and willing and also to enjoy their work. Many Arabian horse owners remark on how much fun they have with their horse and also on the wide variety of performance work they can undertake. A whole book could be filled with examples, such as the little mare Rizanna (Nazir ex El Zaan) who is typical of many who have given their owners years of pleasure, not only as a riding horse but also as a companion. As her owner summed it up, 'she has given me more pleasure than any other horse I have ever known. Not only in the form of winning in several different spheres, but also for her complete loyalty and quite obvious devotion to me over the years.'

A remarkable instance of an Arabian adjusting to a completely new style of work was demonstrated by seven-year-old Harkem, by Haroun out of Sun Dance, for he was chosen to carry a disabled rider in a demonstration at the Third International Conference for the R.D.A. in 1979. David Trexler, a double amputee veteran of the Vietnam war, was coming over from the U.S.A. and had asked for an Arabian, preferably a stallion, that would carry western tack. Harkem had been broken to the hackamore and stock saddle as a four year old but had since been a hunter, Pony Club mount and show horse for his owner's daughter – a complete contrast to the finer points of a western reining horse, which David wished to demonstrate. Only three weeks were available for training and Harkem had to learn to spin, slide and stop and work in a very collected manner with the lightest of contacts on the hackamore, and to take his cues from a touch of a dressing whip, for David had lost both legs from above the knees. In addition he had to be 100 per cent safe with a wheelchair as David, having developed great compensatory strength in his arms, mounts and dismounts from one unaided. That Harkem learned all this in three weeks, including calm acceptance of the close proximity of so strange an object as a wheelchair, was a remarkable feat. David showed superb horsemanship, and the tremendous reception they both received for their demonstration was richly earned. After that little digression Harkem slotted back into his life as a family horse!

Young riders

In Australia the majority of Pony Club members ride Arabians or part-breds. A much higher proportion of pure-bred colts are gelded in Australia than is the case in Europe, and they make excellent mounts for young people competing in all kinds of gymkhana games as well as in the more serious events.

One outstanding pure-bred gelding in the U.K. was Rondhani (Ahram ex Rondetta) who was acquired for 13-year-old Serena Whittaker as a Pony Club mount when he was eight years old. He had had no competitive experience but learnt so quickly and showed such promise jumping that they were soon included in their Pony Club show-jumping team. Going on to eventing, Rondhani proved a brilliant performer cross country; his wins included Henbury B.H.S. Horse Trials in 1990, Cheshire Rose Bowl P.C.

Serena Whittaker competing across country with Rondhani.

One-Day Event, and no less than three times winner of East Cheshire P.C. One-Day Event; he also represented the Pony Club at the 1991 show-jumping championships. Rondhani was the overall Ridden Champion at A.H.S. Haydock in 1988, the A.H.S. pure-bred performance horse for 1991–2, and won the Dinsdale Memorial Trophy for the most versatile pure-bred in 1992. He was a brilliant hunter and a much loved horse, who to quote Serena has 'a great heart . . . is an absolute delight to ride . . . each time I ask him for more, he always responds with his best'. It is difficult to imagine a better mount for a junior rider and he was a splendid advertisement for the breed.

Many other pure-bred geldings, and mares, have been very successful Pony Club mounts. There was Kayal Ibn Ferdi (Ferdi ex Rosehue) who had raced four times before going to 14-year-old Amy Boswell; his exceptional jumping ability led him to be a popular choice for jumping lessons with Y.T.S. pupils at a local riding school. He competed in open competition show-jumping and eventing with much success and also in Pony Club events, having the second best score at the Area 7 One-Day Event in 1989. Shulan (Blue Shugrotto ex Mymalanda) began to be ridden by 12-year-old Amy Downie when he was eight years old and after doing well in ridden classes started show-jumping and dressage, being highly placed in 1990 in Riding Club and Pony Club One-Day Events at both novice and intermediate level. Elizabeth Kipling had great fun with her pure-bred gelding Golden Orient (Blue Orient ex Cranleigh Taimar) competing in Pony Club Tetrathlon, in which they qualified for the National Tetrathlon Championships in 1990. In addition to winning the under-17 title for the second time at the British Modern Pentathlon Championships and the under-20 category, they were chosen to represent Great Britain at the Junior Modern Pentathlon World Championships in Hungary. The previous year they were eleventh at the French Championships.

Mares make excellent mounts for junior riders too. One such is Rasmiga (Gaymet ex Radsilla) who, ridden by her owner's grand-daughter, Samantha Stevens, then aged 13, was shown under saddle in 1989 to win the Young Riders class at the A.H.S. National Show; they also took part in show-jumping at Malvern. They have competed in Pony Club hunter trials and one-day events and in addition had some fun at a Pony Club camp practising polo.

The list could go on and on, but it is only possible here to mention these few. Suffice to say that the future lies with young riders and to see so many of them enjoying a wide variety of activities with Arabians, and with part-breds, is both good publicity and a healthy sign of the breed's popularity.

An attempt has been made in this book to give a brief history of Arabians

ABOVE *Rasmiga and Samantha Stevens in the show jumping at Malvern in 1989.*

RIGHT *Joanna Bailey with her part-bred Beechnut Coffee Cream, by Kalib out of a Welsh mare, second in the 150 mile E.H.P.S. Spirit of Sherwood Ride, 1991.*

171

and their derivatives as horses for performance and, by giving details of some of the most successful, to put on record their ability to hold their own in competition with other breeds.

Last but not least, for all those which appear on public occasions there are a great many more who are simply 'pleasure' horses. They are equally important, because the majority of riders do indeed ride for pleasure, and no breed can give more than the incomparable Arabian, with his need for human companionship, his willingness, toughness, and enjoyment of his work.

Bibliography

Archer, Rosemary, Pearson, Colin and Covey, Cecil, *The Crabbet Arabian Stud, its History and Influence* (Alexander Heriot & Co., 1978)

Brown Edwards, Gladys, *The Arabian War Horse to Show Horse* (The Arabian Horse Trust of America, 1969)

Bryant, Arthur, *The Great Duke* (Collins, 1971)

Fisher, John, *Eighteen Fifteen*

Guedalla, Philip, *The Duke* (Hodder & Stoughton, 1949)

Halambros, K.M., *The Byerley Turk* (Threshold, 1990)

Hyland, Ann, *The Endurance Horse* (J.A. Allen, 1988)

Iman, S.A.H.A.A., *The Centaur*

Longford, Elizabeth, *Wellington – Pillar of State* (Weidenfeld & Nicolson, 1972)

Milner, Mordaunt, *The Godolphin Arabian* (J.A. Allen, 1990)

Riedler, Georg F. and Vreni, *Ethics in Endurance* (Eldric and F.E.I., 1994)

Struben, Pamela, *Horses and Riding in Southern Africa* (Purnell, 1966)

Upton, Peter, *The Arab Horse* (The Crowood Press, 1989)

Vesey-Fitzgerald, Brian, *The Book of the Horse* (Nicholson & Watson, 1946)

Wentworth, Lady, *The Authentic Arabian Horse* (Allen & Unwin, 1945)
    Thoroughbred Racing Stock and its Ancestors (Allen & Unwin, 1938)
    The World's Best Horse (Allen & Unwin, 1958)

Wynmalen, Henry, *Horse Breeding and Stud Management* (Country Life, 1950)
    Equitation (J.A. Allen, 1938)

The Arab Horse Society News (Britain) 1955–95

The Journal of the Arab Horse Society 1935–1938 (Alexander Heriot & Co., 1979)

The Arab Horse Society Racing Yearbooks

Araber Journal – (Europe) (Germany, Austria, Switzerland)

The Arabian – International Magazine (Holland) 1974–6

ELDRIC Yearbooks

Arabian Horse Europe (E.C.A.H.O.) – magazine

The Australian Arabian Horse News – magazine

The Australian Arabian Yearbook

Australia's Crabbet Arabian Horse – yearly magazine (Somerset Publications)

Arabian Horse World (U.S.A.) – magazine

The New Zealand Endurance and Competitive Riding Association Yearbook

Race Arabian (U.S.A.)

SARAB – The Arab Horse Society of South Africa magazine

Index